Willows Weep

MW01286402

Dave Spinks

Copyright © 2019 Starborn Illumination
All rights reserved.
ISBN: 9781695681545

WILLOWS WEEP

By Dave Spinks

Editor: Karen Jurkovic, 1st. Printing
Linda Harkcom, Second Printing

Layout & Graphics:
SJ Designs

Cover Design: Mark Randal

Copyright © 2019
Starborn Illumination Publishing

All Rights Reserved.
1st. printing October 2019
2nd printing March 2021

Table of Contents

Acknowledgements

It has been an amazing journey into the unknown over the last 30-plus years of my life. I have met many like-minded people during that time and have shared many experiences with them. During our journey of life, each and every person we meet has a purpose. Some are just brief encounters and others stay in your life forever. But no matter how brief or how long those encounters are in your life, they have a purpose, a meaning for happening at that particular moment in time. Whether it is to teach us something new, or something old, or simply a chance meeting of two souls traveling on their own journey, in my opinion there is a purpose behind it.

First and foremost, I would like to thank the Creator. I would also like to thank my family for all their support and understanding of what and why I do what I do. Secondly, this book would not have been possible without many people who have dedicated many hours of research and time investigating the house known as Willows Weep and who have shared their experiences from this location in order to tell the story of the house.

I would like to thank Brenda Zimmerman Johnson, the former owner of the house, for sharing some of the most hair-raising experiences I have ever heard in a haunting case and for trusting me with owning this notorious location. I would also like to thank Serenity Jenny at Starborn Illumination Publishing for stepping up and making this book a reality in an extraordinary way on a short timeline. It's amazing when things come full circle. Thanks to my friend Nicole Novelle for contributing her research on the house and sharing her experience when she and I first investigated the house together. Thanks to J. Berman for her experiences in the house. I would also like to thank Brenda's daughter and son- in-law, Tonya and Tracy Cummins, and other family members for sharing their experiences.

Special thanks to Barry Gaunt, Melvin Brazzell and Steve Miller (no, not the musician), of the Night Stalkers team for sharing their evidence and experiences at the house – they were phenomenal. Thanks to Traci Watts and Terri Rhodes for sharing their experiences. Thanks to John and Debbie Holiday who shared numerous experiences that occurred during their investigation of the house. Thanks to Tina and Jackie Hicks for sharing their investigation results from the house. They were the first to ever conduct an investigation of the house and I had the pleasure of investigating it with them as well.

Special thanks to Jeff Phillips for sharing his professional thoughts about the construction of the house and his experiences in the house. Thanks to Brian and Marlena Corns who shared some thoughts and experiences from their investigation at the house. There are many more who have had experiences in this house; unfortunately, it would be quite impossible to include them all.

I must give one person a special thanks for providing her unique perspective about the house -- a perspective that was unlike that of anyone else who contributed to this book. This person spent quite a bit of time in the house. It was fascinating to listen to her perspective of what she felt is going on within the walls of "the Weep". I was in the process of interviewing her for this book, and what she was telling me was quite different from all other accounts and experiences told by others. I am deeply saddened to say she is no longer with us, and our interview was incomplete, but I will share with you her thoughts about the darkness of Willows Weep.

For DOC and Michelle

This book is dedicated to you and Ken "DOC" Head as well as so many others who have spent a lifetime of dedicated research and investigation into the world of the supernatural. DOC was a selfless person who dedicated his life to helping sick people as a doctor. He was a special person and I was proud to call him my friend.

Thanks to Michelle Fitzpatrick for sharing your thoughts and experiences about Willows Weep and your service to your community while working in law enforcement. You will be missed by many in this field and by your coworkers. I want to wish you Godspeed throughout your next journey.

Introduction

"WILLOWS WEEP – CAYUGA, INDIANA"

Over many years of investigating and researching the paranormal, I have traveled to untold numbers of reportedly haunted locations. Most of these locations, have some sort of tragic death, that once occurred on the grounds or inside of the structure itself including: accidents that caused death, suicides, murders, and even human sacrifices.

Many of these locations have proven to have strange phenomena occurring within and around them. Most of these locations are essentially a dime a dozen in the realm of hauntings. However, on rare occasions I have stumbled across a location that makes all the others pale in comparison. A location that has so many tragedies, so many deaths, so many contributing factors, that it sets itself apart from your run of the mill haunted house.

One such location is known as Willows Weep. This house is by far one of the darkest, most spine-tingling, and creepiest houses I have ever investigated. As I learned more about the house, property, history, and the experiences people have had there, I became enthralled about the possibilities this house posed for an investigator of strange phenomena.

I soon learned the paranormal activity is not confined to the house. The property itself is saturated in bizarre, unexplained events reported by many people. As if the deaths that have been recorded in the house are not enough, there are many other factors that, in theory, are conduits of paranormal activity. This location seems to have far more than any I've ever investigated or even heard of for that matter.

For starters, the house is constructed in the shape of a cross that faces east, and a crossroad sits directly in front of it. If that is not bizarre enough for you, let me fill you in on more facts about this one-of-a-kind location. In the middle of the house, in what would be the very center of the cross, four strange points were included in the construction of the four corners of the room, all pointing to the center of the main room of the house. Directly under the center of the main room of the house there is an unexplained fire pit, dug into the dirt of the crawlspace. There are ashes in the bottom of this fire pit and it is surrounded by what appears to be granite rocks. To make matters worse, a young child's arm bone was found buried in this crawl space near the pit. It was taken out and examined and then returned by the former homeowner.

In the front yard, there is a very large and ominous willow tree. It is said by many, that anyone who disturbs this tree, will have an ill fate befall them and there are instances that back this claim up. Very near the house, there are two rivers that intersect with one another, and directly under the land that the house sits on, there is a massive aquifer. The whole area is said to be ancient Native American land. In fact, there are ancient Native American mounds nearby, and there was also a large Native American massacre there. Numerous area residents have said that they often dig up arrowheads and clay pottery when preparing their gardens for the season.

To top things off, while doing a renovation, the former homeowner was removing newer laminate flooring that was water-damaged. It had been laid over the original 1800's floor, and between the new floor and the original floor, the homeowner discovered a strange book in the corner of the room.

This book was published in the 1980s by a strange sect of the Church of God, however the cover of the books sports an upside-down pentagram and the title asks "Is the Spirit world real?" The book itself talks of necromancy, how to communicate with spirits, and how to conjure spirits to name a few of the topics. Now, I don't know where you come from or what your spiritual beliefs are, but no Christian church I've ever heard of would publish such a book.

I had first heard about Willows Weep through word-of-mouth, as I often do, from the many contacts I have developed over the years, while investigating and researching such locations. In 2013, I received a phone call from a fellow investigator, Nicole Novelle. She told me I had to watch a video on YouTube of a location known as Willows Weep in Indiana. Soon after reviewing the video, I decided to look at this location more in depth by reaching out to contacts I have in the field, and researching more information about this property.

I began to hear of investigative teams having experienced some significant paranormal events in the house to include class A EVP's (electronic voice phenomenon), poltergeist activity, shadow figures, doppelgängers and people reportedly being attacked by unseen forces. Full-bodied apparitions had been spotted on numerous occasions inside the house and in various locations around the property.

The more I inquired, the more I was learning just how dark this location is, and to my surprise, this house and property had never been featured on any major paranormal TV show. In today's paranormal world, when a property has a deep dark history, with many deaths involved, the paranormal TV shows are usually all over it without any hesitation. How the house known as Willows Weep had been overlooked up until this point, I will never know.

As an investigator, reports by other reputable investigators should be taken seriously and literally. Little did I know at the time, that information, was just the tip of the iceberg when it came to Willows Weep. I have discovered even more information that adds to the mystery of this house and the people who have lived in it. I would soon experience, first-hand, some very dark and sinister events within the walls of this small, cross-shaped house that sits in the sleepy, little town of Cayuga, Indiana.

I called upon several trusted investigators and researchers in the field who have contributed their experiences and knowledge to this book in order to bring to life one of the most dreadfully haunted locations on the planet.

In this book, you will read real experiences by a former owner, her family members, by myself as well as numerous other well-known and respected paranormal investigators in the field. You will also hear about some of the rumors, that have not yet been proven as factual evidence, but were gathered by neighbors who have first and secondhand knowledge of some of the events that have occurred on the property. These accounts are told as recalled and documented by all involved. I must warn you: some of these accounts are extremely disturbing and may affect you spiritually, psychologically, and possibly even physically. Sit back and get ready to immerse yourself into the dark world of Willows Weep.

CHAPTER 1

THE JOURNEY BEGINS

I began my journey with Nicole Novelle on August 5, 2014, after talking, at length, with the homeowner at the time, Brenda Zimmerman Johnson, about having us investigate the house. Nicole and I decided to embark on journey that included several days of investigations at multiple locations, culminating in the last night at Willows Weep. It would be the first time either of us would investigate the Weep, but certainly not the last. This initial investigation would set me on a course that I could never have imagined.

After investigating the first two locations as planned, we packed up our gear and headed down Interstate 70 toward the finale of our, unprecedented at the time, three-locations-in-three-day, paranormal road trip, Willows Weep. We were flying high with the results so far, because we had captured some phenomenal evidence and experienced some eye-opening and downright creepy things at the previous two locations. Our goal was to launch into three very active and dark locations in a 72-hour time frame, going live at each location. As far as we knew, this had never been attempted before. If it was, it had not been documented in any known, public format.

So far, our trip was a success and we were both ecstatic about what the third and final location may hold in store for us. In the back of my mind, I was feeling a bit apprehensive about having Nicole enter, what we believed to be, the darkest location out of the three. The night before, Nicole had been so severely affected by a negative force, that I was forced to pull the plug and end the investigation a bit early. Something had taken her over to the point that she was incoherent and disoriented. I pulled her out of the house immediately and had her recite prayers. As this was happening, she began to dry heave violently for several minutes. Her eyes looked dark and sunken in, and I was worried for her safety as well as my own. After approximately 30 minutes, she began to snap out of it, and I began to feel relieved. We packed our gear and called it a night.

The next day, as we traveled closer to the location, we talked about the events of the night before. I wanted to be sure that Nicole felt ok and that nothing from the events that took place the previous night was affecting her. She assured me that she felt fine, and that she was ready to proceed to the final location. I was slightly reassured, but still couldn't help but wonder if this negative force was following us or if it would rear its ugly head at the next location. I couldn't help but wonder what we may have stumbled into.

CHAPTER 2
THE ARRIVAL

The Upside Down Cross Shaped House

As we neared our destination, the GPS showed we were only a few miles away. As we traveled down the state four-lane, the GPS told us to turn off, on to what seemed to be a one-lane country road right through the middle of a massive corn field. The corn had not been harvested yet and was at peak growth. It was impossible to see anything except corn in all directions. After a mile or so, we still did not see any sign of a house or civilization for that matter. We began to think the GPS had led us astray. We chattered back and forth to each other, wondering where in the hell we were. I couldn't help but wonder, "Was an unseen force manipulating our GPS?" We began to discuss turning back and getting back to the highway, when we entered a slight curve that led us to a beautiful old covered bridge with a restaurant in front of it. The small river and bridge were beautiful. We couldn't resist stopping for a look. After all, it was a very old bridge and the history of locations is one of the reasons we do what we do. Every location has a story and now we were a small part of it.

We walked up the bridge, admiring the history. Built in 1873 by a man named J.J. Daniels. It was a quick photo op, and back in the car we went and continued our journey towards the house. According to the GPS, it was only about a mile down the road. We came to the spot where the GPS said the house was, only it wasn't there. We looked around very carefully for several minutes continuing to look for the house. We began to wonder "Was something paranormal affecting our GPS?" Getting frustrated, we turned the GPS off and reset it.

Finally, we were able to find the house. The first thing we noticed was the huge weeping willow tree in the front yard. It towered above the house and its long, full-blooming branches hung all the way to the ground. It was a beautiful tree and did not look intimidating to me at all. We had both heard some of the lore about this tree and, not wanting to tempt fate, Nicole was extra careful skirting around the branches that hung into the driveway. She parked the car. We climbed out, stretching with excitement, ready to unload our gear, set up and start the investigation.

Our first task was to prepare for the radio show we were co-hosting at the time. But first we had to meet the owner. We waited around for a little bit to see if anyone was there and no one was, so we headed next door to Z's house where she lived at the time. We knocked on the door and Brenda said she would be over in a few minutes. We headed back over to the barn that sits directly behind the house. The barn is a modern structure that is fairly large. I would guess that it is at least 30 feet wide by 40 to 50 feet long, with a metal roof and sides. We talked between ourselves about how much time we had to set up for the radio show and began to get our game plan together. That's when we noticed Brenda making her way across her yard toward us.

Brenda opened the door to the barn and we followed behind her. The inside of the barn was not what one would expect. To the right, there was a pool table and two beautiful Harley Davidson motorcycles. In the far-right corner was a full-size tiki bar. There were all kinds of pool tournament trophies and plaques that covered the right-side wall and sat on shelves. As I looked around, while Brenda and Nicole were making small talk, I noticed all the trophies had Brenda's name on them. I blurted out, "These are all your trophies Brenda?" She said, "Oh, yeah." I said, "That's impressive." Then I noticed that she had pictures of some of the biggest names in the professional pool world, including her. Obviously, she was at one time a professional pool player. I thought, "Wow that is really cool."

I made my way over to Brenda and Nicole, and began surveying the rest of the barn. It had some older furniture in the back-left corner, a large commercial sink in the left front, and an older stove, along with a bunch of cooking-related stuff on shelves. Brenda began to explain that she and her family often have cookouts and picnics in the barn. This made perfect sense, it was set up just for such a thing. She asked if we wanted a quick tour of the house. We both said of course. Up to this point, I hadn't felt anything negative or unsettling about the place.

CHAPTER 3
THE WALKTHROUGH

Brenda led, and we followed her out the barn door. Just to the right there was what looked like a storage shed built out of brick and was roughly 6 foot. wide by 8 or 10 foot long. Brenda opened the door and explained to us that the building was the old summer kitchen that was used for many years back when the house was built. She said a lot of the teams use this building as their control center. I poked my head in and noticed that everyone who had previously been there to investigate had signed their name on the large white plywood that was hanging on the walls. She said, "You guys can use this or the barn for your gear. It's up to you." We then continued back toward the rear door of the house.

There was a large padlock across the door and Brenda explained to us that she wouldn't be awake when we were done. "So just lock the door on your way out," she said. We went in the outer door that led into a very small mudroom with a hot-water heater, a few small shelves, and another door. Brenda opened the inner door that led into the kitchen, explaining to us that this door will often open by itself, with no explanation, and that she and others had captured this on camera numerous times. Nicole and I looked at each other with raised eyebrows as we entered the kitchen.

Just to the right, was the doorway, leading into what I would describe as a living room. I noticed that there were electrical cords running along the floor, coming in through a dryer vent hole in the wall, and they were connected to a few security cameras that Brenda ran constantly in the house. We proceeded into the living area, and Brenda began to point out things to us. First, she said, "That is the chair that the last man who lived here died in. He shot himself in the bathroom, stumbled around and came to fall into his chair where they found him two days later." I stepped closer to have a better look and, to my horror, the chair was covered with what looked like blood. I asked Brenda if this was his blood, and she said, "Yes, it is." I was shocked that this was left in the house. I asked why it was still here, and she told us that the guy's son didn't want any of it and just sold it as is. "He wouldn't even come into the house with us when we looked at it, and we never took it out during renovations due to all the things we had been experiencing every time we tried working on the house," she told us. Without missing a beat, she said, "And over here, in this corner, is where we found the book with the upside-down pentagram on it buried between the old floor and new floor." The hairs on my neck began to raise up and a cold chill went down my spine.

The air in the house was very thick, and you could feel the heaviness begin to engulf you. Over to our right there was another door that led into a very small bathroom. She walked over to it and said that's where the old man was found dead. After his wife died in the house, he became a hermit and lived in the bathroom until he died.

Brenda continued moving towards the center of the house where a large archway led into the next area. The shape of the house was now taking form to me. It was shaped just like a cross. We followed her into the center room as she began to explain more about the house. She pointed to the ceiling, showing us the four large points in the corners, that are built into the structure of the house, and all pointed to the center of the room where we were standing. She explained how they discovered those while looking for the staircase that was in the original building plans of the house. Instead of the staircase, they discovered a false ceiling, which they took out, exposing the strange points. No staircase was ever discovered leading up to the attic.

She explained that originally there were four exits and entrances in the house and all four of them were in the corners. Those were all closed in and little extensions had been added over the years. Now there were two entrances and exits, the front door that was added to a new front porch area and the rear door that we had come through when we entered the house through the kitchen that was added sometime in the early 1900s. She stood near the big archway that we had crossed coming into the room and told us that, according to an elderly neighbor, a young man had hung himself right in this area in the 1950s.

She then moved into the room off to the right and took us to the east wall of that room, where she showed us a strange burn mark on the wall that resembled a bull's head with a blob for a body. She said that right at that spot, there had been a large cross that hung on this wall. She went on to explain how one day they had come into the house to do some work, they found the burn mark on the wall and the cross was very mangled, lying on the floor. She also told us that this was the room, where the last woman who lived here overdosed. The woman was the wife of the last man who died in the house by gunshot wound to the head. During my research, I discovered that she was pronounced dead of heart failure at the local hospital. Her family claims that she died in the hospital, even though I have an eyewitness, who was a neighbor and friend, who claims to have seen the emergency crews wheeling her out of the house covered up with a sheet. They eyewitness said the emergency crews were not attempting lifesaving procedures on her, which would lead me to believe she was no longer living when they wheeled her out of the house on the gurney. The eyewitness also claims to have lived there since the 1960s and knew the couple very well. I find it hard to believe that this person would fabricate this account, having nothing to gain from it. So for now we will call the woman's death associated with the house.

I was looking around in awe at the structure while listening to Brenda talk. Each room had 8 to 10 feet tall, double doors, made of solid wood, that were original to the house as were the heavy, thick floors. Just then, she noticed me looking at the doors. She explained that she had security cam footage of those doors opening and shutting on their own, with no one being in the house at the time, not only once, but numerous times. "I would love to see that footage," I chimed in. She said sure. She pointed over toward the room on the left and said, "Step in there and look at the right-side door." I walked in and turned to my right. Immediately I noticed that door's inners were shattered and split to pieces, some still hanging attached to the door, some completely missing. I asked, "What happened to this one?" She said that it had slammed so violently, back and fourth, one time that it shattered the inner part of the door. I replied, "Holy shit!" She remarked that it was happening so often, they had gathered some large rocks from outside, that weight at least ten pounds, and placed them at the base of each door to keep them from slamming and destroying any more of the doors. She said, "But that doesn't even stop them. I have video of the shutting with the rocks on the floor and it had happened when teams were in there to witness it." I was even more intrigued to see the footage of this.

She continued with numerous tales of unexplained phenomena occurring to her and her family as well as to investigators in the house -- everything from physical attacks to poltergeist activity as well as these things trying to kill her and her husband. She pointe out where and explained when these things happened throughout the house. We were now getting behind schedule, so we ended the walkthrough with Brenda, and headed back toward the car to begin the tedious task of setting up our equipment.

The original plan was to start off our investigation with the live radio show, that Nicole and I were co-hosting together at the time, broadcasting from the Weep. Then we would conduct a live investigation of the house, on my YouTube channel, for the rest of the night.

We got our gear set up inside the house. As we began testing our Wi-Fi signal in the house, it seemed that it would be sufficient to conduct the live radio show as well as the Investigation. We conducted the radio show by phone, then decided to take a bathroom and dinner break before starting the live investigation, but first we wanted to do a test of the live feed before leaving. Soon it was apparent that something did not want us to livestream from the house. Scrambling around, trying to figure out what to do to boost our signal, Nicole decided to run to the nearest store, which was 20 miles away, to obtain a Wi-Fi signal booster so we could go ahead and livestream the investigation. I decided to stay behind and get everything charged up while she went to the store.

After about an hour, she returned with the booster and we hooked it up to the Internet box that was in the barn out back. We began to livestream and it appeared to be working fine at first. Within five minutes, we began to experience a lot of electronic interference and buffering. We began to troubleshoot, and could not figure out why we could not livestream the investigation. After an hour or two of racking our brains, as we worked feverishly with much frustration, the decision was made to forget the livestream and simply film it. It is important to note that, during this time, we were experiencing unexplained noises inside the house while we worked. At the time, we were concentrating on getting the live feed to work. Only after the investigation was over did we realize that the activity inside the house during all of that was high, almost as if someone or something was affecting our electronics inside the house.

We began the investigation by setting up various flashlights in the house and just talking out loud to whomever or whatever was inside the house. We asked the entities to only turn the lights on and off when we asked them to. Using the flashlights in an investigation is highly controversial due to them being fallible. However, if I use flashlights at all these days, I use at least three of them. All three are different colors, and I attempt to get the spirits to turn on different ones by asking them to manipulate them by the color. The odds go up significantly that it may be something, paranormal in nature, manipulating these flashlights if one can get a specific color to turn on and off upon request.

Nicole was sitting in a chair and I was manning a camera as one of the lights turned on by itself without any provocation. Nicole, without missing a beat, asked for it to turn off the light because we had not yet asked anyone to turn it on yet. The light began to blink and slowly turned off. She thanked whatever it was and asked, "If you are the person who built this house, please turn on the light." Immediately the same light turned on and went back off. She thanked this unseen thing again. She then asked again,"Just to confirm -- if you were the person who built this house, please turn on the light again." Nothing happened at first. She then asked one more time, with me chiming in as well, saying, "We just need confirmation -- If you were the person who built this house, please turn that light on one more time." The light came on immediately. Now we were possibly getting somewhere as to who or what might be in the house. We asked many more questions using the lights and nothing else significant was captured.

Later in the investigation, I had finally gotten the live feed to work on my channel, and we were using a hack shack ghost box. Before we even asked a question, as I walked by the ghost box, an old woman's voice came out of the box saying, "That's the one, Dave." As if to single me out for some reason. Was this a premonition from the spirits in the house, that they knew then, more than four years beforehand, that I would one day be the owner of Willows Weep? A minute or so went by and another woman's voice came from the box and said, "Take both of them," as if they wanted to attack both of us or attach to both of us. I finished what I was working on, and decided to move near the table the ghost box was sitting on to conduct a session. The first thing I asked was, "Who was turning the light on and off? Tell us your name please?" A woman's voice responded immediately saying, "Don't know," followed by a growly male voice saying, "Me." We know that a man, who was a postman, had built the house in the late 1800s. Was this the man's spirit answering us through the ghost box?

A child's voice then came through the box and it was inaudible. I proclaimed, "I do not think you're a child. I think you're something that is acting like a child." Just then a growly man's voice, the same voice as before, came through the box and said with authority, "That's right!" The energy was changing in the house to a very creepy feeling, as if something very negative in nature was gaining strength. As I said this out loud, multiple voices called out in a row over the box, "Help, backroom, leave," followed by yet another voice saying, "Front room." We know we were getting multiple voices, coming from the box, asking for help, sounding as a living person would sound if in duress or in a warning state. The energy was really ramping up at this point. Just then the live feed shut off. I shut the ghost box off and asked out loud, "If that was any of you messing with the electronic devices, can you make a loud knock or bang right now please?" Immediately we heard a faint knock, followed by a very loud thump. This was fascinating as well as a bit creepy, realizing that something you can't see, is intelligently responding to what you are asking it to do on command. I then realized that whatever was in the house with us may have been gaining energy from the electronics we were using, and it was affecting the devices to the point of them shutting down and losing power. We both called out to the spirits of the house to please not touch us or mess with the electronics, hoping that they would listen to us.

Out of thin air, the faint sound of a child humming was heard by both of us. We continued trying to elicit further communication with what is in the house. I asked it to knock one more time. The device in the other corner came on. I responded, "We know you can turn the light on, but can you do another knock for us?" As I was saying this, I got the knock I asked for. The energy was beginning to get a bit overwhelming for me. I could feel my energy being drained. That little voice in my head was screaming at me to get out of there and take a break but another part of me was saying, "no, you can't leave" because the communication we were getting was insane at this point. We began to experience multiple unexplained taps, thumps and knocking noises coming from all around us. I noticed Nicole's demeanor changing and I could tell she was being affected as well. It was then we decided to take a break.

During our break, we discussed what to try next. I wanted to give Nicole a little more time to regroup, especially after what she had experienced at the other location the day before. I suggested that I go in by myself and do a session to see if the energy would be any different with just me in there.

I decided to use the hack shack ghost box again. I began by saying "I want to talk to the spirits that like to hurt people in this house. Can you tell me your name, please?" An immediate response of "Baphomet" came from the ghost box. This sent shivers down my spine, but I didn't react negatively because, if the entity that was in the house was truly a demonic spirit of some sort, I didn't want it to think it scared me in any way. I asked, "Was this house built so that you would have more power or energy on this plain?" A clear voice from the box said, "I hope so." I switched gears and began trying to communicate with one of the reported suicide victims in the house. I asked, "Is the man who hung himself here with me now?" A few seconds went by and man's voice said, "I'm here." I then began hearing all sorts of different voices coming through, as if many spirits were trying to speak to me. Normally this happens with this type of ghost box; however, here at this location, the box wasn't receiving any radio bleed over. The only thing coming through during the previous session was white noise and static. I was getting some of the best ghost box responses I have ever gotten at this point. The responses were immediate, clear and intelligent to the questions I was asking. I ended the session and went out to see if Nicole was ready to re-enter the house.

We decided to continue with the hack shack due to the responses I was getting during my solo session. As we started the session, an unprovoked response came over the box saying, "Ask them." I replied, "Ask who?" A clear response of "Brenda" came out of the box. This was compelling since the owner of the house at the time was Brenda. I then asked, "Who's the boss in this house?" A very clear response, in a deep growly voice, came from the box, "SATAN." I shuttered a bit hearing this response. I quickly shrugged it off knowing that sometimes human spirits will play games with you, trying to scare you. I kept my guard up and continued asking questions. I made a bold statement, telling the nasty entity in the house that if it was controlling the human spirits in this house it needed to let them go. As I was saying this, I was moving around a bit and that's when I felt a violent force hit the floor beneath my feet, lifting me up a bit, at the same time a cold burst of air went right through me from the floor moving in an upwards direction. This startled me, and I said, "Holy shit!" at the same time the ghost box spit out the word "demon" in a woman's voice as if to warn me that's what had hit the floor under me. Instantly my entire body became cold. To me this was a sure sign that a negative spirit was trying to affect me and was attempting to manifest itself in the room with us. I exclaimed very loudly not to touch me. Just then the hack shack said, "Touch him" in a female's voice. That's when Nicole called out not to touch her either. Hearing this, I called out that I do not give you any permission to touch me.

The energy in the room was now palpable -- very thick, very heavy -- and the air was cold all around me. We decided to shut the hack shack down in the hopes of decreasing the energy it was putting out. I started asking questions out loud to see if we could garner other responses. We asked questions to any human spirits, and asked them to make a knock or bang to let us know where in the house they were hiding. We continued asking other questions as the knocks and bangs started to come from several different locations, from above in the ceiling, from the rooms around us and from under the floor. As this was happening, Nicole said it felt like something stabbed her in the back. We tried not to acknowledge this at the time to give it any more power. We kept asking questions ,as the bangs persisted all around us, for approximately 30 minutes.

We switched gears once again and began to use another device that spits out words based off the EMF that is being picked up near the device. One of the first words it typed out was "Bassago." I relayed it to Nicole, so she could do a quick search of the word and it came up as being the third demon referenced, in the lesser king of Solomon. It then said the word "devoured" followed by "splatter." This was astounding considering that a man named Jesse Sykes was actually eaten alive by his own hogs on the property. With his entrails hanging out and various parts of his body missing, including part of one of his feet and an ear — due the pigs eating them — his family carried him back into the house where he bled out and died. A truly horrible way to die. The other word, may have pertained to the last person to live in the house, who tragically shot himself in the head. It was uncanny to us how many relevant intelligent responses we had obtained during the investigation from numerous paranormal devices.

It was getting very late and we were both physically, mentally, and spiritually drained from the negative energy that was flowing through the house. As we packed our gear and began to load up the car for the night, I was in the room where the bloody chair sits, winding up an extension cord, when a massive force hit the floor with a tremendous thump sound, once again moving me just a bit. I jumped back, cursing at the top of my lungs, foolishly yelling at the invisible force to stay away from me and not to touch me. I took this as a warning that we had pissed whatever this entity was, and it wanted us out of there. We wanted to continue, but knew it was time to finish this one up.

We were ecstatic with the results of our first investigation at Willows Weep. It had lived up to its dark reputation and then some. However, it is one of those places that the activity is so intense that you are left wanting more and that, can be very dangerous. It becomes like some sort of addiction. As an investigator, you become so involved with it you can let your guard down, becoming enthralled to the point that you can set yourself up for gaining an attachment. We both knew that we had just scratched the surface, and that one day we would return to document the paranormal activity that persists at Willows Weep.

A few days after we returned home, Brenda informed Nicole that a team had come in the very next night right after us. They reported to Brenda, that they had captured the name Nicolle numerous times ,over the course of their investigation, on various devices. The asked Brenda if anyone named Nicolle had died in the house. She told them no, but the night before we were there. "There was a guy and woman here and the name of the woman was Nicole," she told them. To us there was no coincidence in that.

CHAPTER 4
THE RETURN

Little Girl Footprint

I wouldn't return to the house for more than a year. During that time, I had met Tina Hicks and Jackie Mossberg Hicks at a paranormal conference in Indiana and soon struck up a friendship with them. They invited me to be a guest at their upcoming conference and I accepted. We had chatted about investigating together in the future. I asked them about Willows Weep. They told me about some startling evidence they had captured there — a few years before I had ever investigated the property. They explained that they had gotten permission from Brenda, to sprinkle baby powder on the floor, to see if they could document the powder being disturbed by something unseen. While sitting in complete darkness for quite some time while investigating — never moving or walking around after spreading the powder — one of the people with them, said out loud, that something had touched his leg. Turning on the lights, to their surprise, there was a set of footprints in the powder. The prints appeared small, like a child who was not wearing shoes, had walked right past them and disappeared into the wall.

This story intrigued me greatly. I had been itching to return to the Willows Weep house, and I decided to call Brenda and book it once again. I figured this would be a prime opportunity to investigate with the The Original ParaSisters®, Tina and Jackie. I called them up, and the date was set: Halloween night 2015.

I arrived early in the evening and met with Brenda. She began to fill me in on some of the new happenings at the house. She exclaimed that investigators had been witnessing a lot of shadow figures, and people seemed to be getting attacked on a more consistent basis. She also said that, since I was last there, she had shut the house down for several months due to the severity of some of the attacks that had been perpetrated on her and members of her family as well as on some of the investigators who had been to the house. While the house was closed and no one had been in it for quite some time, she told me, on numerous occasions, she witnessed the curtains opening and shutting from inside the house, as if someone was looking out the windows at her while she worked outside in the yard. I finished talking with her and wondered what was in store for us later that night during our investigation.

We went into the house and my plan was to livestream from the house once again. The cell service looked great -- three bars of 4G -- and that was plenty to have a decent quality stream from the house. I started up, the live feed on my channel, by introducing myself as I always do, and then I introduced Tina and Jackie. Almost immediately, the live feed started to freeze and buffer. The cell service should have been plenty to do a live feed. Since the first time I had investigated the house, I had talked to numerous other investigators, and it seemed to be the status quo at Willows Weep, to have unexplained electronic device failure. This night seemed to be par for the course. I decided to just do the best we could with the live feed and record the whole thing for quality footage on my channel.

We began by the ParaSisters® scanning the entire house for any abnormally high EMF fields. They walked the entire house without finding a single anomaly. We decided to move on using a ghost box very near the bloody chair. Before I turned on the box, we were talking about the live feed, when all three of us heard a child-like voice say something. We stopped in mid-sentence and confirmed with each other to see if we had all heard that. It was a fact, we all had heard the talking at the same time. I turned on the ghost box and before I could even get a question out, a girl's voice came out of the box saying, "Leave, Dave, and get out." I sat on the arm of the chair and asked, "Whose chair is this?" A man's voice said, "Mine." I asked, "Why did you shoot yourself?" A response in a man's voice replied, "Bitch!" I was stunned. I said, "You did it because of your wife then?" A clear and resounding, "Yes" in the same man's voice chimed in from the ghost box. This response was very eye-opening. Could it have been, that he was so grief-stricken from losing his wife, that he couldn't live without her? Or, could it possibly have been, that some dark force took advantage of his grieving state and manipulated him into committing suicide? To me, these were both plausible explanations as to why a man would take his own life. During my session, I captured the name of the man, who died in the chair, several times, while standing right next to the chair that he was found dead in. The word demon was also captured several times during my first session near the chair.

We moved into the main room, and I handed the box off to Tina, to see if we could have a woman communicate with any possible female spirits in the house. As she was asking the woman in the house to say her name, a woman's voice said Tina's name. She asked again to please tell me your name? A clear woman's voice came from the box and said the name "Maria." As they began to get responses on the box, while standing in the center room of the house, Jackie said the whole floor was shacking as if we are standing right next to train tracks. This seems to be a very common occurrence in the house when the energy begins to ramp up, as I encountered this sensation on my prior investigation, along with many others. As we continued into the ghost box session, a man's voice called out my name once again. The box was going crazy, with several voices coming through. There was a distinct child's voice coming through, a man's voice, and a couple of different women's voices, all seemingly talking at once. All at once, another woman's voice came out of the box and she spoke the name of the last woman who overdosed in the house. They continued trying to communicate with her for more than 30 minutes with no further response from her.

As the session was progressing, I noticed the live feed was buffering again, so I began to work on it. I called Tina over to help me with it, and she passed the ghost box off to Jackie who stayed in the middle of the room, while we worked on the signal. Upon review of the video, while Jackie was standing in the middle of the main room, she had pulled out a pendulum to work in tandem with the ghost box. As she did this, a very quick burst of light shot right towards her hand that was holding the pendulum. Within a second, the pendulum began to swing in a circular motion on its own. This was compelling because, we were all standing in pitch darkness, and she never saw the light anomaly that went right towards her. This evidence wasn't even discovered until much later, when the footage was being reviewed. She asked it to stop and it did. She then asked for it to move in a back and fourth motion and the crystal began to move back and fourth ever so slightly. She quickly thanked it and put the pendulum away. It appeared to me when reviewing this footage, that she was slightly unnerved by what was transpiring.

At this exact moment, we had just gotten the feed running smoothly. Tina returned to the main room and took over the ghost box once again. Within a minute of Tina taking over the session, a man's voice said Tina's name loud and clear. She responded, "Oh my goodness." Jackie and I both confirmed that we had heard her name as well. She quickly asked, "Who just said my name?" A quick and clear answer soon came out of the box. The name Tina came out of the box three more times, within a few minutes, in a couple of different men's voices. Then Tina asked, "Who else is saying my name right now? You know my name but I don't know yours." A deep growly voice said, "Sykes." This was now getting insane. Sykes was the name of the original family that built the house and lived in it for a few generations. She walked over to the room that has the demonic-looking burn mark on the wall and asked, "Whose room is this over here?" A sharp response of "Mine" was heard by all of us. She asked, "Yours?" She also noted for the camera that it was very cold in this room. No other significant responses came from the box while in that room. Tina moved back to the main room, standing in the center, still holding the ghost box. Once again, the live feed began to have problems. I was beginning to get very aggravated, but I realized it was most likely due to the energy in the house affecting the electronics. As this was going on, the temperature dropped very drastically in a short amount of time. We decided that it was a good time to take a break.

Once our break was over, it was decided that the women would start off together in the center room, by themselves, without a living male presence in the house with them. As they conducted the session, nothing significant was happening, until Jackie began to see a shadow figure moving around in the kitchen area. As she stated what she was seeing, the floor under their feet began to vibrate significantly. Then voices began to come out of the ghost box, telling them to leave and get out several times. Another voice came from the box saying, "The portal's open." Just as all of this was going on, Jackie began talking about how uncomfortable it is in the house because of the shape of the house. She was describing how you don't feel safe in here because you can't put your back to anything and you're left wide open. Just as she was talking about this, I had returned from outside and began to talk to the live crowd that was watching us. In the background, a very clear light anomaly was captured on the camera, moving from right to left about eight feet off the floor, very near the front center room of the house. Many other investigators have reported seeing a large shadow figure in this area as well as numerous light anomalies. This remained unknown until I reviewed the footage. As I continued talking to the live viewers, all three of us saw a quick flash of light in the room with us. This was the third time this had happened during this investigation. We all felt as if there was something attempting to manifest itself in the house with us. I finished addressing the live crowd and started setting up the next session. The ParaSisters® sat on the couch as I prepared the equipment. We began hearing noises coming from the room behind us.

I finished setting up the equipment to start the final session of the night. I had planned on using a new device for this session, however the device would not turn on at all. It was fully charged earlier in the day and was put aside with the power turned off completely after taking a full charge. It appeared the Weep had drained yet another electronic device.

I decided to run another ghost box session. I began by asking any spirit who wished to communicate with me to say my name. Immediately a male voice responded with the correct answer of "Dave." I proceeded to ask it to say my last name. Two separate distinct male voices responded,

"Spinks." I tried to go a step further by asking, "Can any one of you spirits say my first and last name together?" One of the male voices said, "Dave." After waiting a few more minutes with no further responses to those questions, I moved in another direction. I asked if the man who died in the chair was still here with us. A clear "Yes, here" came out of the ghost box followed by a voice saying his name. The phrase "think about it," also could be heard, as if another spirit was telling him to think about it before he answered my question. To me this was an amazing exchange. Speaking directly to him, I asked, "Can you tell us again why you killed yourself?" A clear response of, "Love" was heard by us. As I tried to get more confirmation pertaining to the reason why he shot himself, a different voice came across the box and said, "Choke, choke." This was a bizarre response because it didn't pertain to my line of questioning. At the time, people in Brenda's family had reported being choked in the house. Was this a warning or a threat that something wanted us to cease what we were doing? Just then, we heard three loud thumps in the house. A startling response of "Check, her" came out of the box. This was very interesting since the response used the name of the woman who overdosed in the house. I ran with it and asked if she was here with us? A clear female voice answered, "At the morgue." I didn't know if it was the woman who overdosed in the house or another female confirming that her spirit was at the morgue. I asked once again, "Are you here?" A man's voice answered, "She's dead."

As all of this was going on, I saw a white flash of light on the wall, behind Jackie's head. As I was alerting them to what I had just seen, I asked, "Are you behind Jackie?" A completely different female voice answered, "Right behind," confirming what I had just seen a few seconds earlier. During this time, the energy in the room with us was very electric, and we were astonished at the amount of intelligent responses we were hearing from the hack shack. I wanted to go another route at this point. I turned the box off and said, "Ok, let's try this" and I asked, out loud, for whoever was just behind Jackie, to make a noise to let us know they were here with us. Just as I finished saying this, something tickled my hand. This startled me, and I lurched backwards explaining what I had just experienced. I asked again,

"Whoever is behind Jackie please make a loud noise." We waited for a minute or so with no response.

I went back to the ghost box. The first question I asked was to the woman who had overdosed in the house, "Are you still here with us?" A clear response in a male voice said, "She's with her husband somewhere." I thought to myself, "Wow! this is insane." I jumped up and grabbed one of the husband's hats from his chair to use as a trigger object. I held up the hat in one hand, as I was holding the hack shack in the other hand and I asked, "Is this yours?" A clear man's voice said, "Yes." I then asked, "What is it that I'm holding in my hand?" A clear response of "a radio" from a female voice answered me. Although this was not the answer I was looking for, it was a clear, intelligent, factual response because I was holding the hack shack radio in my other hand. It was a mind-blowing response! I reiterated the question by saying, "No, not in that hand, the other hand." There was no clear response. After several seconds, I asked, "Is this your hat? Yes or no?" After several more seconds, we heard a very faint response of what sounded like, "It's mine." I replaced the hat on the headrest of the chair, where it has always sat since the man's death. I decided to hand the box off to the ParaSisters® as I tried to process the series of events that had just transpired. The sheer number of intelligent, factual responses was immeasurable.

As for me, I was satisfied, at this point, that the house was definitely occupied by not one, but several intelligent spirits. The sisters decided to try and communicate with the wife again. Tina asked, "Did you feel hopeless?" A very low response was heard saying, "Yes." After several more questions to her, with no direct responses, Tina asked, "Are there people buried under the house?" A childlike voice answered, "Yes." Jackie then asked, "How many are buried under the house?" A clear response of "five" was heard. This was startling to me because of the child's arm bone that was found under the house — by Rocky the maintenance man — several years earlier. Not to mention that, we got the same response of five, much earlier in the investigation. All of this, adds to the mysteries that are yet to be uncovered concerning the house and its dark past. The ParaSisters® s continued and asked again to get confirmation, "So, there are five people buried under the house?" Not one, but three distinct voices replied, "Yes." They asked, "Can one of you speak with us?" They both asked numerous questions with no significant responses, until the question, "Did you live in the house?" was asked. A female voice answered, "Yes." We continued for 30 more minutes with no further significant responses. As we were continuing to ask questions, Tina reported seeing a shadow figure behind me in the room, and they both reported that they did not feel right in there.

After having experienced so many different things, including: unexplained thumps, bangs, shadow figures, light anomalies and a plethora of intelligent ghost box responses throughout the entire investigation, we were feeling content with the investigation. We decided to wrap up our very active, and intriguing investigation at this notorious haunted location in Indiana. As with many haunted locations, I knew I would be back. But this one was different. It was proving to be more than just one of those locations with unexplained knocks and bangs. This one seemed to be alive with intelligent spirits, topped off with something lurking behind the scenes that was very dark. This was my second investigation at the Weep and it hadn't shown itself to me yet. I didn't know when I would be back, but I knew there was much more for me to try and uncover here.

CHAPTER 5
THE BIG DAY

I continued investigating many locations. Myself, along with fellow investigator David Weatherly, had become extremely busy with many projects, events and investigations with the Society of the Supernatural. Though we conducted numerous investigations together, throughout Indiana, we had never investigated Willows Weep together. I would often bring it up to him, but we had so many other locations lined up in Indiana, that it just never transpired. After more than a year had gone by, with countless other investigations under our belts, an incredible opportunity came up.

It was the summer of 2017 and I was on vacation with my family in South Carolina, when I got a call from Nicole Novelle, the first person I investigated the Weep with. She was nervously excited and explained to me that our friend Brenda was going to have to sell the place. Nicole said that Brenda told her she was done with the house because she truly felt it had tried to kill her and her husband. I sat there stunned, listening to this, wondering what all could have happened at this dark location. I knew that her husband had some health issues, but never imagined it was from the house. Nicole went on to explain that Brenda told her that she didn't want to sell it to just anyone. Brenda told her she felt either Nicole or myself were the only ones that could handle the Weep, even though she had several other people interested in buying the place. I asked Nicole if she was going to buy it and she explained that she was not in the position to at the time, and said that I should buy it. After talking with her for quite some time, we hung up and I pondered the situation.

I knew that owning a dark location such as this was a daunting task. There would be numerous investigators wanting to investigate the house, and that comes with all kinds of liabilities. There was also an inherent danger to being the owner of such a location. Brenda, her husband and numerous others in her family, had been attacked by dark unseen forces in and around the house. If I purchased the Weep, I would be subject to similar attacks. I knew all too well, the possibilities of being physically, mentally, and spiritually attacked in a home, even while investigating one of these dark locations for long periods of time. I had already been through a similar situation when back in 2013-2014, when I participated in an unprecedented investigation, at a notorious haunted house, at a location known as the Wells House in Wilkes-Barre, Pennsylvania. I, as others involved in that investigation, lived in it for more than 30 days during one stint. I was involved in three more stays, in that godforsaken house, for at least a week and a half or more each time. Upon leaving that house, I had the worst year of my life. I discovered there was a large, cancerous tumor in my leg that only appeared directly after the investigation, and my financial situation was dire, due to an impending divorce, that only started during my investigations at that house. But that is another book, for another time.

Needless to say, I had some major concerns about owning the Weep. After weighing my options, I felt it would be a chance like no other, to study paranormal phenomena at my own leisure without any interference, fees, or regulation.

While talking to Brenda on the phone, I asked her why she felt she needed to sell the house, and why she was adamant that either Nicole or I have the house. She explained that the house, or whatever is in it, has tried to kill her husband twice now and continually has caused her and her family too much pain. It was time for her to sell. Brenda was so disturbed at what had taken place with her husband, herself, and her family, that she packed up and relocated more than 20 miles away, just to be away from Willows Weep. She also said that she chose me or Nicole, as the two main possible buyers, because she truly felt that we were the only ones strong enough to deal with it. She said she knew that we would make sure things are done the right way, and that we had already recognized it for what it truly is, a place of pure evil and despair. We came to an agreement on the price. A date was set, to announce that I would be the new owner/caretaker of the house, during a meet and greet, in August of 2017.

I was excited but concerned. Did I just set myself up to relive a similar experience that happened to me while in the house in Pennsylvania? Or even worse, could there be some weird connection between the darkness in Pennsylvania and the darkness that lurks in the Indiana house? Was that same darkness drawing me into it once again, by causing certain events to happen, that led me into owning this haunted location? Only time will tell if this is the case, and I will have to deal with it when the time comes, if it turns out to be true. I also knew, that I had a prime opportunity to own my own place, that could be utilized as a paranormal lab, so to speak. I knew I would most likely never get another chance like this, and I knew in my heart that it was the right decision. I had a vision for this property. As I explained before, this house is one of a kind. There is nothing else like it out there, and the tragic history and paranormal activity needs to be told and shared with the world. As an investigator, this is what it's all about — to try and document evidence of the paranormal phenomena. There are thousands of investigators out there, attempting to do just that. However, to own my own location, as an investigator, is a dream come true and there aren't many people out there who can say that.

I could hardly contain myself waiting for the day to arrive, that it would be known, that I was new owner of Willows Weep. I had planned to attend the meet and greet incognito, as a guest speaker with a vending table. Once the event was about to start, Brenda would announce that I was the new owner of the location.

I had a plan and now it was time to implement it in phases. The first phase would be for me to investigate the location as the new owner and that I must say was a bit unnerving. I didn't know what to expect. I was in uncharted territory now, because even though I had investigated many hundreds of haunted locations over many years, I had never owned one. I had no clue what to expect. After all, I wasn't just investigating the house as I had before,I was now investigating it as the owner. This was a whole new experience for me. I had conducted several hundred investigations over my time as an investigator, but never as an owner of an extremely dark location. I had previously lived in a very dark location, for a total of at least eight weeks, and I had suffered greatly from that one, in various aspects of my life, for an entire year afterwards. Now I had become an owner of an even darker location. What would become of me now? Would I be attacked as Brenda's husband was? Would a negative spirit cause me to have a heart attack or stroke? Would I be scratched, or choked, as others had previously been in the house? The only way to find out was to investigate.

I planned on arriving Friday night to set up my table and do an investigation with some of Brenda's family members in the house, before Saturday's meet and greet. I believed that doing the investigation, with some of her family members in the house that had been attacked, may provide me with some insight into what darkness lies within the house. As I drove from West Virginia, I planned in my head, some of the questions I would be asking that night, not only with Brenda's family in the house but as the new owner. This was something very new to me. I had investigated several hundred locations in my 30-plus years of paranormal investigations, but never as an owner of one. I was in new territory. Would the dark forces turn their anger and attacks towards me now that I was the owner? Would they, instead, lash out one last time at Brenda's family, or would they do both? Only time would tell. As I drew closer to the house, my heart rate began to climb. I was both nervous and excited to be at this location once again, only this time it was different -- now I was coming as the owner. My demeanor was that of pure adrenaline as I could hardly contain my emotions. All I could do was crank up the music in my car and jam out to level myself out.

I pulled into the driveway, careful not to disturb the willow tree. Some members of Brenda's family, who were staying in a camper for the event, were out in front of the barn. I pulled up and began to chitchat with them a bit. We discussed the Weep awhile before I went next door to

Brenda's old house, where she and some of them were spending the night before the next day's event. We talked for a lengthy amount of time and I asked her if she wanted to attend the investigation with me later. She said, "No way in hell" she was going to do that. I knew that would be her answer due to all she had been through in the house, but out of politeness I was obliged to offer.

It was time to investigate. It would be me, Brenda's daughter, her husband, a cousin, and a couple of the older kids who wanted to investigate the house. I wasn't too hip on the younger kids being involved, but if the parents wanted to let them check it out, I couldn't yet say I was against it, quite simply because the house wasn't officially mine until the next day.

CHAPTER 6
INVESTIGATING AS THE OWNER

I wanted to keep it short and simple in order to try and minimize the amount of time the family spent in the house. I wasn't sure what to expect with having them inside the house during an investigation. Some of them had been attacked in the past and I did not want that to happen again. I gathered up: a recorder, REM Pod, a full spectrum go pro, Mel Meter, and hack shack ghost box. Once everyone got settled into their seats, Brenda's daughter, and her husband, shared some of their stories of being touched and seeing unexplained things in the house on numerous occasions. I wanted to start off with the ghost box to try and get the energy flowing in the house. On previous investigations I've conducted in the house, the spirits seemed to be very responsive with this device with many quality and relevant responses. I was very anxious to see what kind of responses and activity I would capture, with some of the family members in the house — who had been attacked inside the house on previous visits.

The first question I asked was, "Who is in here with us?" The response was, "Brenda." That was interesting, because Brenda just happened to be the former owner and I was in the house with several members of her family. I tried to get more information by asking who had said the name Brenda, but there was no response. I realized I didn't form the question directly enough, so I asked the question, "Are there any human spirits in this house?" The response was "All kinds." A second response of "patient," followed by "evil" came out of the box. I didn't hear the third and fourth responses while I was conducting the session and only discovered these during the review of the audio. I repeated the question, "Are there any human spirits in this house?" A woman's voice answered, "girl." Attempting to get more information, I asked for the name of the girl. A deep, growly man's voice said, "GET OUT!" Almost immediately, a completely different woman's voice came out of the box saying, "I didn't get out!" As if it was talking to the deep, growly voice that told me to get out. This was getting very creepy. At this point, we had heard four distinctly different voices come out of the ghost box and one of them seemed to be talking to the other deep, growly voiced man who didn't want us in there. This is not unheard of in the paranormal realm while conducting ITC sessions, but it is also not very common.

I was beginning to realize that the spirits that lurk in the Weep may be much more intelligent than I even realized. By all appearances, it seemed that not only could they interact with the living, but they were also interacting with other spirits that resided in the house.

I continued with the session by asking, "Is there an evil force or presence in this house?" A strong male voice said, "It's in there." I followed up with, "What was this house built for?" A whispery voice responded, "necromancy." Followed by "future." This response was absolutely mind-blowing because of the book, that was found hidden in the corner of the room, where the last man died in the house. This book was found between the original floor and new laminate flooring during some early remodeling Brenda and her family had been doing. The book was distributed by an offshoot of the "Church of God," which in the 1980s, resembled more of a cult than an actual "Christian organization." This book gives general information on how to communicate with spirits and even has a section that deals with "necromancy," which specifically means, according to *Webster's Dictionary*, "the supposed practice of communicating with the dead, especially in order to predict the future (witchcraft, sorcery, or black magic in general)."

Without evening asking the next question, a woman's voice came out of the box, giving a dire warning to all of us. It said, "This place is evil!" It sent a cold chill through my entire body. Before I could get another question out of my mouth, the same voice came over the box exclaiming, "They're coming!" It was getting very intense. At this point, I was trying to wrap my mind around what had just transpired in the first five minutes of the investigation. I decided I would hand the box off to one of the family members and see what kind of reactions the spirits would have communicating with them. I wanted the spirits to choose who they wanted to talk with, so I went and stood in front of each person, one at a time, and asked "If you want to speak with this person, say yes or no." I went over to the first person and asked, a quick, "NO!" was heard. So I went around the room asking the same question. When I got to Brenda's daughter the response was, "Sure." Needless to say, she got to hold the box and continue the session.

I went over to the couch and took a seat to observe what kind of interaction was about to take place. She was feeling very uncomfortable and wanted to hand off the box right away. I convinced her to keep going. The box was saying, "Leave" and "Get out" constantly, without her even getting out a question. We asked, "Did you worship Satan?" A quick answer of "Yes" came from the box and that did it for her. She handed the box off to her husband. Before he even got started asking questions, as he was standing in the very center of the house, a female voice said, "BEEZLE." Could this be referring to the demon Beelzebub? Theological sources, mostly Christian, say that name is simply another name for the devil, the same as Satan. He is known in demonology, as one of the seven princes of hell. This response seems to be a common one in some of the darkest locations I have investigated. The response is always chilling to hear coming out of any device we use as investigators. Getting this response, is by no way proof, that the devil or even a demon is manifesting in the location. It could simply be a human spirit, warning you of what they perceive to be an evil presence or force. Nevertheless, it is still unnerving to hear.

Brenda's son-in-law didn't hear the response, nor did any of the others, because there was no reaction by any of them after the response. I heard it very clearly, but I chose not to react to it. I did not want to alarm them. He finally got out a question. He asked, "What was the guy's name who killed himself?" The response clearly said the man's name, followed by "yeah." Another direct, intelligent and factual response. He asked, "Is he in here with us now?" A direct, clear "Yes" came from the box. All the while Brenda's son-in-law was conducting his session, I could hear numerous voices coming out of the box saying, "Leave," "Get out," "Satan," "evil." It was uncanny the amount of negativity I was hearing. I kept silent, choosing not to acknowledge those voices for the moment. Personally, I like to listen for direct responses to the questions that are being asked. For me, that is better evidence than just random words coming out of whatever device is being utilized at the time. All though, you can't overlook that amount of negative, almost warning-like words, coming out of the device at a feverish pace.

He asked, "Is there a woman here who killed herself?" A clear "Yes" and "angry" came out of the ghost box. I decided to chime in with a couple of questions. I asked, "Did some negative force cause those people to kill themselves?" Not one, but three, different voices answered, "Yes." I went further and said, "Was that force conjured here by spells, or witchcraft?" A clear response of, "religion" was heard. This was getting very real now. He asked, "Do you want anyone else to hold the box now?" A very clear response of "Elaine" came out. It so happened that one of the family members, in the house with us, was named Elaine. Wow, I thought to myself, another clear and intelligent response.

Elaine got the box and prepared to start asking questions. Before she started, I asked the others if they were all ok, because I was still feeling light-headed and dizzy, since I stood in the middle of the room holding the box. A couple of them said they were not feeling quite right. I told them if anyone of you feels uncomfortable or sick, to not hesitate to get out of the house. I knew there was something amiss taking place. Everyone chose to stay, so we continued with Elaine holding the box. I followed up with my next question and asked, "Is there anyone buried under this house?" A response of what sounded like a number comes out of the box. I thought I heard this, but wasn't sure, so I asked a more specific question, "How many bodies are buried under the house?" Upon reviewing the footage at a later date, I discovered that I did hear a number and it was seven, which was a perfect match to the clearer and second question. This was an excellent piece of evidence. Getting confirmation of this sort, is very exciting. A very clear and quick response of "seven" was heard. It was a bit unnerving to hear this. As we were repeating the number seven, which we all heard very clearly, another voice using the box plainly said, "Could be eight," like it was in the room with us, having a conversation. I can assure you, it was no living person in the room with us. Wow, I thought to myself, we are communicating with something extremely intelligent.

I know for a fact, that a very old child's arm bone was found by Rocky, under the house. Immediately after uncovering the bone, in a pile of dirt under the house, he was violently attacked by an unseen force. Brenda pursued all avenues, trying to find out what should be done with the bone. She was instructed by local law enforcement to either get rid of the bone or return it to where it was found. She decided to return it to its resting place, under the house. I had to ask myself, was this the prelude to discovering more body parts under the house, or even worse, entire skeletons of deceased persons. Nevertheless, more investigation into this matter is warranted and will most definitely be pursued by myself in the future.

As the session continued, a strange light anomaly was captured on the full-spectrum camera facing the couch. This anomaly, was approximately one foot off the floor, on the right-hand side of the couch, moving towards the camera, and appeared be self-illuminated. Upon closer inspection of the capture, it appeared to have a tail-like appendage, that seemed to be flowing as it traveled steadily towards the camera. The whole occurrence lasted approximately ten-seconds and no one in the room noticed it at the time. As Elaine continued asking questions with the hack shack, she asked if the bodies were sacrifices. A clear response said, "Yes! To the devil." It was a downright disturbing response. Elaine asked, "How many of them were children?" The response was "four." My heart sank hearing that response, especially knowing a child's arm bone was found buried under the house. Just about then, I got a pounding headache and I knew something was trying to affect me in the house.

We switched gears and asked for the woman, who overdosed, to give us her name. No response was captured. I then said, "If you give us your name, I will give you a pill. Would you like that?" A clear woman's voice replied, "I suppose." This was an intriguing response. Of course, I didn't have any type of narcotic pill. But I would have gladly left an aspirin for the spirit. I followed up by asking, "What kind of pill was your favorite?" A female voice answered quickly and clearly, "hydros." We all were blown away and repeated what we just heard come from the box. It is well known, that the word "hydro," is a slang term or short for hydrocodone, a well-known synthetic opiate that is derived from codeine and is a favorite of drug abusers. It is ingested orally or by smoking it, snorting, and it is even used intravenously.

We were having a phenomenal session, so we continued. I asked, "Are you the woman who overdosed in the house?" A response of "No" was heard. This was a bit disappointing since there is factual evidence, from a close friend and neighbor of the couple, who saw the woman being wheeled out of the house deceased, confirming she died in the house. Within a few seconds of the "No" response, out of nowhere her name came from the box. I was elated because I now felt that the first response, was from another spirit, that was communicating with us at the same time. Now we have received a clear response, with a known person, who overdosed in the house. This, to me, is paranormal gold. There was no doubt in my mind we were communicating with something intelligent, that couldn't be seen. I couldn't say, without a doubt, it was the spirit of the woman who overdosed in the house, but with what was being captured, it was leaning a bit closer in that direction.

I still wanted more information. I wanted more confirmation. The responses were like my drug. The excitement of what was transpiring was intoxicating. I asked, "Is your name _____?" A clear, woman's voice answered, "Yes." Oh my god. We all went silent for a second and then we erupted "Yes!" It was now clear to me that we were communicating with the spirit, of the woman, who overdosed in the house. I was covered in goose bumps from head to toe. What was great about it was there were eight other people in the room, all of whom witnessed it, and experienced it themselves. All were in agreement as to what was happening. I wasn't finished yet. I wanted to connect the dots even further. I asked her, "What did your husband do to himself in this house?" The same-sounding female voice responded over the ghost box, "shot." I shivered with excitement and realization, that I just got even more confirmation, we were dealing with a highly intelligent force.

One of the men asked, "Did he shoot himself in there?" pointing towards the room, where the bloody chair still sits to this day. A few confusing responses by a few different voices said: "Yes" in a man's voice, "Yes" in woman's voice, "No" in another woman's voice, and "Yes" in yet another woman's voice. I said out loud to the group, "Wow, there are multiple spirits communicating right now."

Initially, most thought he killed himself in the chair he was found in. However, upon interviewing Brenda's husband, he told me that he had talked to one of the police officers who was there during the investigation. He said the police figured the man had actually shot himself in the bathroom. However, the shot didn't kill him and he stumbled out of the bathroom coming to rest in his chair. That is where he bled out and died. He was found two days later. Was the response by the man, confirming the police's theory as to how it all happened? Makes one wonder is all I can say.

Brenda's son-in-law Tracy — her daughter Tonya's husband — jumped in and asked, "Is that the last man to die in the house's chair in there?" A deep man's voice answered clearly, "Yes," followed by "Yes, shot." It was insane the amount of intelligent factual responses we were getting during this short investigation. Going back to the woman, I asked, "Why did you overdose on pills? Was it an accident or on purpose?" A female voice said, "drunk." This was eye-opening, and it made sense to me. It could have been a total accident. She may have had one too many alcoholic drinks, mixed with some pills and she never woke up. I'm not saying that's what happened, but it's a plausible explanation. We asked the same question again to her and for her only to answer, "Was it an accident or was it on purpose?" Not one but three distinct responses replied, "accident." Bingo. That was enough confirmation for me.

The energy seemed to be changing in the room now and it began to feel darker in nature. Without our even asking any questions, a woman's voice said, "Satan." I ran with it. I asked her if she was being influenced by negative or demonic forces. A quick answer of "Yes" came out of the box. After several more questions, pertaining to a dark force influencing her, no responses were captured.

I went back to the man and I asked, what kind of gun did you use? I heard a very light voice say, "Colt." I have no information, to confirm or deny, what brand of gun was used at this time. I then asked, "Was it a pistol, rifle, or shotgun?" A fast response in a man's voice said, "rifle." After that response, the energy changed again, and a response of "demon" came from the box, without a question even being asked. I rolled with it again. I posed the next question to the couple. I asked, "Did either of you practice any black magic or spells in this house ever?" A man's voice answered right away, "No." I followed up and said, "Were you being possessed by an entity?" A clear response of "Yes" was captured. I asked several more questions with no responses.

Moving into a different line of questioning, I asked if the house was built to funnel energy in and out. An immediate answer of "Yes" was captured. I then decided to say, "If there is a negative spirit or demonic in this house, I am going to ask you a question and you will be able to understand me." I asked, "Como te llamas?" which is Spanish for "What is your name?" No response. I asked again, this time with more force, saying, "In the name of God, como te llamas?" An immediate response of "Satan" chimed in from out of the box. I cannot say for sure that the response had any truth to it or not. However, it was becoming more apparent, that something in the house was indeed negative in nature and was attempting to intimidate us by using that name. I was feeling the negative energy becoming more intense. I instinctively had begun holding my cross in my hand and didn't even realize it at the time. It was when I reviewed the video, that I noticed myself, holding the cross between my fingers. What happened next, made me realize that there is definitely a powerful, negative force in the house.

As I gripped my cross, I asked, "What am I holding in my hand right now?" No immediate response was heard. About 15 seconds went by, and this response came from the box, "Fuck you whore-cross." We did not hear the full response audibly. All we heard was the last word, "cross." Upon reviewing the audio and video, the whole response could be heard. Whatever responded was clearly, really pissed at the object and me for wearing it. These are some of the signs we look for when dealing with negative type entities. There was no doubt in my mind now. I asked, "Do you like this symbol?" A growly masculine voice said, "Take it off!" We all heard it and we're even more stunned now.

Many voices started coming out of the box. The voices were becoming more negative and growly sounding, and I realized it was becoming dangerous. I didn't want anyone to be attacked in the house. I immediately stopped the session. I went to turn on my fully charged flashlight and it was dead. It was truly, one of the most actively, intelligent investigations I have ever conducted. I knew now, without a shadow of a doubt, that this house and property were the real deal.

As I was grabbing up my gear to take it out of the house for the night, my head began to pound even harder, and I had a severe pain building in my left foot near my big toe. I knew all too well what this was -- it was the beginnings of gout in my foot. The first time I ever got gout was at Bobby Mackey's during an investigation. It is another notorious negative location. I have had gout only seven times in my life. Four out of the seven times, were during an investigation at a haunted location. The other three times, occurred shortly after I returned from an investigation. I can't say this is paranormal-related, but it's awful coincidental. I have also experienced the loss of my voice on three separate occasions, while en route to and at the Bellaire house in Ohio. In my opinion, due to numerous experiences, it is my belief, that these unseen spirits can and will affect you physically.

I learned a great deal during my first investigation as the new owner of Willows Weep. I feel the house was the most active to-date for me. Having members of Brenda's family in the house with me, may have been a catalyst, along with me, now becoming the owner, may have contributed to an elevated level of activity. This was just the first step, in long journey that I am on, to try and unravel the mysteries of the house. I have much more work to do. I will be bringing in very well-known investigators, from a variety of backgrounds and experience levels, to get their take and experiences on the property and house in the future. For now, I am convinced that there are multiple intelligent spirits attached to the property along with something very ominous in nature lurking there.

The following day was the meet and greet to introduce me as the new owner of the house and property. During the event, Brenda and I gathered everyone into the barn for the announcement. Event-goers and family alike, all sat and listened intently, as Brenda proclaimed I was the new owner and caretaker of the Weep. I watched the crowd's faces; some were stunned, some were happy, and some were sad. I thought to myself, "Am I going to get backlash from certain people, especially from the ones that felt they owned the house, and had taken advantage of Brenda for several years?" No matter. I knew what I had to do, and I was going to do it.

Brenda called me up to the front and turned it over to me. I explained my vision for Willows Weep to the onlookers. I talked of how this house should be known, as one of the most haunted locations in the world, and that I was going to make sure that happened. I went on to explain how I was going to turn it into a paranormal laboratory, with limited human interaction, due to it being very negative in nature.

At the conclusion of my speech the barn erupted in applause and I felt really good about where this was going. I knew that, with my contacts in the field, I could bring in some of the most respected people to investigate the home — many of whom have vast experience and insight — to help bring this haunting to the forefront of paranormal research. They would be free to make their own determinations, as to what was haunting the house and what could be some of the possible causes behind the paranormal activity. It was all going to be in the name of research to advance the field.

CHAPTER 7
BRENDA'S INTERVIEW

BRENDA & DAVE OUTSIDE WILLOWS WEEP

The following is taken from an interview with the former owner of the Willows Weep house in October of 2017. I have known Brenda, since 2014, when I investigated the house for the first time. She is a no-nonsense type of woman. I believe, what she experienced in the house, is real and that those experiences have affected her life in many negative ways. She is a good-hearted person who is very giving to her family and friends. She is a God-fearing person, and even though she presents a tough outer shell, I believe she has a heart of gold. She is also one heck of a cook.

Brenda bought this house in 2010, seven years before she sold it to me. During the interview, Brenda stated, that her son lived in Illinois and wanted to move closer to his mom. While looking for a house for her son, she came across the house now known as Willows Weep. During the search, she claimed that she kept coming back to the Willows Weep house, for no known reason other than she said, "There was just something about this house."

While inquiring about the house, she met the former owner's son at the property, to inspect the inside of the house. The man's father, the former owner, was the last person to live and die in the house — he had committed suicide in his home by shooting himself in the head. Upon entering the house with her son, Brenda looked backed at the former owner's son, who would not enter the house. He told Brenda that he wasn't coming in and wanted nothing to do with the house.

Soon after buying the house, while working on the inside of the house, things began to happen. There was a wood two-by-four leaning against the wall. Brenda claims the wood flew in mid-air across the room and struck her son in the mouth, leaving him injured. She said saws would move across the floor by themselves.

The floor in the main room was buckled due to being wet, so they decided to remove the new laminate flooring. While doing so, they discovered a strange book between the floorboards, in the corner, near the main door that led into the center room of the house. The book seemed to be an instruction manual on how to communicate with the spirit world. The book has a pentagram on the front of it. Thinking this was very strange, Brenda and her family kept working on the house. They soon noticed that the main room of the house is shaped very similar to pentagram.

Later on, as the family had gathered to help work on the house, Brenda's, then 3-year-old, niece asked if she could go into the house. Brenda told her "No way," but she allowed her niece to look in the window of the house, from the outside. Suddenly, the little girl asked, "Who's that man in the house?" Brenda said, "I don't know, I don't see anyone in there." The little girl described the man she saw as having long hair and a beard.

Another incident that took place was soon after, involved an eight-year-old boy name Brent who was visiting. Brent was playing on a bar which was located between two of the trees in the yard, next to the house, when he suddenly came running into the garage area yelling, "Oh my god, I just saw Jesus Christ." They asked him what he was talking about, and he replied that there is a man at the door in the house and he looked just like Jesus Christ. The boy claimed that he and the man kept staring at one another. Soon little

Brent became scared and started running toward the garage. As he ran, he looked back over his shoulder and he saw the man fade away into nothing.

Brenda claims every time she or any of her family had gone into the house, something paranormal in nature has happened. One such incident occurred when Brenda and her cousin were in the house. As her cousin was sitting in a chair, an invisible force, picked her cousin up by the neck and dragged him up the wall behind the chair with his feet dangling. The force then let him go, falling back into the chair. Her male cousin weighs more than 200 pounds.

Brenda claims that her husband was a nonbeliever when it came to any sort of paranormal happenings. That was until, on one occasion, when he was with her in the house fixing things, and he witnessed a man and a little girl walk through one of the walls of the house. Soon after this encounter, when her husband would enter the house, he began having excruciating chest pains, so much so that Brenda had to take him to the hospital. He had to have a pacemaker installed. Before this incident, Brenda's husband had no major health issues.

Much later, Brenda's husband went back into the house, and soon after, he started having severe headaches. The headaches were so intense he couldn't get out of bed. Brenda, worried about her husband's health and called an ambulance. Soon after arriving at the hospital, her husband became unresponsive, and it was discovered that he had three brain aneurisms. Brenda said each time her husband comes to the house he becomes very ill. She said the house or whatever is inside it is "pure evil."

The last time Brenda went into the house was soon after I bought it from her. She said she had gone inside the house to retrieve her security cameras and she will never go back into it again.

It wasn't just Brenda's family that experienced the strange goings on at the Weep. Rocky the neighbor and caretaker was hired, by Brenda, to help her place floor jacks under the house because parts of the floor supports were in bad shape. Brenda had told Rocky, as he was going under the house, that there was a six-foot-long mound of dirt he would need to clear a path through to get back under the area of the house where the floor jacks needed to be placed. She handed him a long stick, to help him wipe the mound of dirt away, to make his path.

While clearing the dirt away, Rocky noticed what looked like a large bone appear in the mound of dirt. As he wiped it away, he grabbed the bone and quickly crawled out from under the house, to show Brenda his gruesome discovery. When he handed it over to Brenda, he was visibly shaken and made the comment that he would never go back under the house.

Brenda took the bone to a local doctor in the area and he confirmed that it was, in fact, a child's arm bone from the elbow down. Not knowing what to do with the bone, Brenda reached out to local law enforcement, who instructed her to either get rid of the bone or return it to where it was found. Not knowing what to do, Brenda quickly returned the bone back to where Rocky found it, reburying it under the house where it still lies today.

On another occasion, Rocky was under the house, working on things, and he claims that he was sexually violated by something under the house. He will not give details of the attack, but it was evident when talking with him, that what happened to him, affected him to such an extent, he will not go into the house to this day.

Another incident Brenda recalled with Rocky, happened when she and Rocky were painting the outside of the house. They couldn't reach the tallest part of the house, so they pulled a pickup truck next to the side of the house and put the ladder in the bed of the truck, to reach the height they needed. Rocky was on the ladder painting, more than 20 feet high off of the ground, and Brenda was in the bed of the truck holding the ladder to keep him stable. As Brenda was holding the ladder, it began to shake violently and quickly became uncontrollable. Brenda yelled for Rocky to get down off the ladder. As he began to descend, something threw him off the ladder to the ground some 20 feet below, landing on his back. Brenda asked him if he was all right. Luckily, he was. Brenda decided she would go up and try to finish painting that area of the house. She got up to where she could reach to paint, when she heard a woman's voice say, that she was going to push Brenda off the ladder. Brenda said she was thinking to herself, that she was just being paranoid, due to what had just happened to her friend. So she shrugged it off and started to paint, when the ladder unexplainably slides two feet to the side with her on it. Brenda said that's when she decided to get down and get down fast.

The willow tree in the front yard is very treacherous. Brenda had warned Rocky numerous times not to do anything with the willow tree. On one occasion, while Rocky was taking care of the front yard near the willow tree, Brenda was in the driveway near the garage. She saw a van stop on the street in front of the house and back up very fast and stop. So Brenda went to the front of the house to see what was going on and she saw Rocky lying on his back near the neighbor's fence. He was conscious and awake. Brenda asked him what had happened and he replied that he was unable to move and he couldn't feel his legs or anything. She asked him if he cut the willow tree. He said, yes but that he had just made one clip on it and it threw him across the yard. He was taken to the hospital where he learned that his back was broken.

One other occasion, a friend Brenda's, along with two others, were visiting. Before they left, Brenda had warned them not mess with the tree on their way out. Being a non-believer in such things, one of the men decided to tempt fate. As the three of them backed out of the driveway, the man reached out, grabbed a branch of the tree, and cut it off, placing it on the dash of the car as they left. According to Brenda, a few hours after the three men left the house, while doing 80 mph, they went off the road, ran into a cemetery and hit a tree head on. All three men had to be life-flighted due to severe, life-threatening injuries including: a broken back, necks, and one leg twisted completely around in the wrong direction.

Another disturbing incident, dealing with the willow tree, occurred when a woman, who had lived with the man who shot himself, came to visit the house, shortly after hearing of his death. She asked Brenda if she could go in the house. Brenda, feeling sad for her, said that she could go in and help arrange the furniture and stuff in the house. Later, she went out near the willow tree for quite a while. The woman asked Brenda if she could please take a branch of the willow tree home with her. Brenda advised her that it was not a good idea, but if that's what she wanted to do, to feel free. Leaving the woman to her own devices, Brenda went back to working on the other side of the house. Eventually the woman left. Approximately a month later, Brenda got a call from out of state, where the woman was living, telling her that the woman had died suddenly, under mysterious circumstances, at the young age of 37.

While having dinner in the garage area, that doubled as a family gathering point, Brenda's granddaughter Emily, who was three at the time, was waving at someone. One of the family members said, "Who is she waving at?" Brenda turned around, to see who her granddaughter was waving at, and saw no one. Brenda asked her, "Who are you waving at?" Little Emily said, "The little girl up in the window, Nana. Don't you see her?" Brenda saw nothing. A few seconds later, Emily started screaming in pain, saying that the little girl had bitten her on the face. The family watched in horror as the bite marks appeared on her face. The little girl and her family are petrified of the house and will not go back to it.

Brenda said there were many occasions when the house would be closed and locked up for months at a time, with no one in or out of it. She said she would always keep the curtains pulled shut during these times. Brenda said, on numerous occasions, she would be out in the yard doing work and would see the curtains open. She said she would hear banging and screaming coming from within the house, as if the spirits were trying to get her attention.

Another disturbing fact about the house, according to Brenda, is that there have been numerous people who have visited the house over the years and at least seven of them have tried to commit suicide, shortly after leaving the house. One of these people happened to be Brenda's niece, who had never been in a haunted location before. The niece and her boyfriend where in the house, attempting to communicate with whatever was in the house. While using a recorder, they got the name of Kendra. Upon playing the recorder back, the niece came running out of the house in a hysterical manner and locked herself in the truck. The boyfriend, concerned for her, attempted to get into the truck, but she had locked the door and was proceeding to take handfuls of pills trying to kill herself. The situation became an emergency very quickly. The police were called while, Brenda gained access to the truck and struggled with her niece to get the pills out of her mouth. Luckily, a tragedy was avoided in this instance.

Several married couples have attempted to sleep, overnight in the house, in one of the beds. All of these couples have divorced and some have even lost their kids, after tempting their own fate within the house.

A neighbor, who has since passed, told Brenda, that in the 1950s a woman who had lived in the house had three husbands die mysteriously, and the woman also had a young daughter who went missing, never to be found. The woman who lived in the house also had an older son, who it was said, hung himself in the archway between the main room and the room that the bloody chair now sits in.

According to Brenda, there is not just one spirit in the house, but many. She also claims, when someone is buried in the cemetery across the street, those, who have gone into the house that day or soon afterwards, will capture the person's name on a recorder or other paranormal equipment such as a ghost box. She says it's like clockwork because it has happened on many occasions since she's owned the house. Further confirming that, the house, may contain a portal or portals, that draw in spirits to it.

Inside the house, in one of the bedrooms, there is a burned spot, that mysteriously appeared on a wall. It just so happens, that the burn mark, is shaped similar to what a horned demon may look like. It also just so happens, that the exact spot where this mysterious burn mark appeared, was the exact spot a cross had hung on the wall. Brenda feels that the demon that resides in the house, burned itself over top of the cross, where it once hung on the wall.

Brenda also claims that once, while inside the house, this demon showed itself to her, face-to-face, in the bedroom where the burn mark appeared. She also said this demon smelled of rotten flesh.

On another occasion, a known psychic named Dalton Croft, came to the house and drew a picture, for Brenda, of what he saw in the house. At the same time, he had Brenda draw a picture of what she came face-to-face with, in the bedroom with the burn mark, while she was outside in the garage. When the two pictures were compared, the pictures were said to match up in many ways. Dalton also stated he felt as if the demon, in the house, was marking its territory.

During the interview, I asked Brenda how many times she felt that she had been attacked in the house by something unseen. She recalled the first time happened, while she and several members of the family, were working inside the house. They were all sitting around, taking a break, and she noticed that her back began to have an extreme burning sensation. When they checked her back, she had six giant scratches from the top of her back all the way to bottom.

On another occasion, she was having visitors over to the house and she was standing in the middle room, when she suddenly felt as if something stabbed her in the back. She looked around to see if someone was behind her, and no one was there. All the visitors were in front of her. In severe pain, she soon left to go to her other house next door. She told her husband that she needed to go to the hospital. She said that something bad was wrong with her and that something had attacked her in the house. Once at the hospital, the doctors ordered a CAT scan and discovered that her kidney was severely bruised. She wouldn't go inside the house for almost a year after this incident. She also reported that, after this had happened to her, others who had gone in the house, also had felt as if something punched them in the kidney and they themselves had to seek medical attention. She went on to say that it's not uncommon for people to be hit in the kidneys and back and have their hair pulled.

The last attack upon her, as she tells it, happened the very last time she entered the house to retrieve her security cameras from the house. She said she went into the house and told the spirits that she no longer owned the house; that she sold it. As she was saying this, her cross on her neck lifted up off of her body, hanging in mid-air by itself, as if something was trying to strangle her with it. She quickly yanked the cross back down. Then a camera cord, that was hanging on the wall, came off and wrapped around her neck three times, in an attempt by some unseen force, to strangle her for a second time. She unwrapped the cord, grabbed her cameras, and quickly exited the house, never to return.

CHAPTER 8
INTERVIEW WITH ELAINE BRANNON

I met Elaine Brannon during the meet and greet the day I became the new owner of the house. She shared, with me, a few of the things she personally experienced while helping Brenda clean the house. I conducted the interview on the same night I interviewed Brenda, the week of Halloween 2017.

Elaine had experienced and witnessed a wide range of occurrences in the house over the time she had been helping Brenda, from some that seemed almost playful to some that were down right frightening to her and others she was in the house with at the time.

Elaine recollected a time when she was sweeping in front of the blood-soaked chair. She said she I noticed the hat, of the man who shot himself and died in that chair, that normally sits on top of the chair, kind of waiver a little bit and then fall down into the chair. "I just turned my head back towards my broom and kept sweeping. When I was done, I put the hat back on the top of the chair where it always sits and I left," Elaine said.

She told me about another time she was sitting, in what they call, the old woman's room and it felt like something was rubbing her back. "And something has played with my hair a whole bunch of times in the house," Elaine said.

Another time, Elaine said that she and Brenda were in the house cleaning, and the wheelchair came out of the room it is kept in all by itself. "It came around the corner right at us and just stopped," Elaine said.

She said that she had also been in the house when fishing poles flew off of the wall all by themselves and she said she is not the only one that had happened to. "Some of the local firemen had come over to the house, and fishing poles, that belonged to the man who shot himself, flew off the wall at them and scared the heck out of them. They left pretty quickly," Elaine told me.

Not all of, Elaine's experiences were that playful. She told me about a time, she was in the front room of the house, with her husband and brother-in-law. The men had come out of the front room and Elaine was still in the room by herself. "The big door with the rock in front of it slammed all by itself. They both screamed for me to get out of there because it scared them so bad," Elaine said.

She told me of another incident, when she and her husband were in the house, and they heard a moaning sound coming out of the side room. "We walked over there, shut the door and it stopped. We opened the door and you could hear it again, but there was no one else in the house with us," Elaine said.

Like many of us that have been in the house, Elaine said she too has also experienced something hitting the bottom of the floors making, her and those with her, all jump a bit.

Elaine was with Brenda when she entered the house for that final time, to get her cameras out of the house after I bought it. She said she saw the cross Brenda was wearing around her neck, get pulled in an upwards direction "as if something was trying to choke her."

"I saw the cord wrap around her neck. Before we even got in the house to get the cameras, we noticed some sort of bone lying on top of the well door next to the kitchen door. I don't know where it came from," Elaine said.

Elaine also seems to have inadvertently caught one of the spirits with her camera. Not long before I purchased the house, Elaine had come over to have Sunday dinner, with Brenda and the family. "I thought it would be really cool to take a picture of the house to put on a T-shirt for the upcoming meet and greet. I took a bunch of pictures of the house. Once I got the pictures back from being developed, we noticed there was a full-bodied figure of a woman in the front window. That's the picture we used for the T-shirt," Elaine said.

Upon examining the picture, I couldn't help but notice the figure bears a striking resemblance to a woman, who is known to have died in the house, Mary Ann Sykes. Mary Ann was born July 13, 1828 and died Dec. 31, 1915. She was the wife of Jesse Sykes. Mary Ann seems to like to appear in pictures, as she has been captured numerous times, by different folks inside the house.

CHAPTER 9
HALLOWEEN 2017

It had been a few months since I investigated the house as the new owner. I was itching to get back to the house and begin the next phase of my journey as its caretaker. I figured what better time to investigate than All Hallows' Eve? I have always loved to conduct a big investigation, at a notoriously haunted location, on Halloween. I have done so, for several years in a row now, each time, trying to go for more days, at crazier locations. Now that I own my own sinister location, I figured this was a must-do situation. The plans were made; the dates were set. I would do four days and five nights of investigating at the house, the final night culminating on Halloween. It was the chance to spend some real time in the house.

Finally, the day came to head to the house. My gear was packed, car fueled up, and I was chomping at the bit to get started. I fired up my Dodge Challenger and down the road I went, thus beginning the next chapter in Willows Weep's history. One of my favorite things to do is drive on the open road. I enjoy seeing new things and going to new places. I have made thousands of drives during my more than thirty years of investigations and, almost always, I end up discovering new things and locations. This time was a bit different for me. Usually, I would be headed to a reported haunted location, owned by someone else, but this time I was headed to my own. It was a completely different feeling. I couldn't help but wonder what the Weep had in store for me.

Day One

I arrived at the house after an eight-hour drive. I was pumped with adrenaline. I grabbed the keys to the garage, went inside, and began setting up my tables and gear for the investigation. Since it was already dark and I had driven all day to get there, I decided I would just do a run and gun investigation for the first night. It would have literally taken me three or four hours to set up all my cameras and DVR system. I grabbed my go bag that I keep ready to go, just in case, I need to respond to a residential or location in an emergency situation. The bag contains: an EMF meter, a recorder, a couple of ghost boxes, and one full-spectrum go-pro camera. I would do a complete setup the next day.

Upon walking in, I did a quick walk around with a Mel Meter, to see if there were any EMF spikes going on. There should have been no EMF readings at all in the house. As I walked around, I began to feel a heavy and negative presence surrounding me. I shrugged it off and proceeded with the walk through. The kitchen registered nothing on the meter. I headed to the room that holds the chair that the man, who shot himself, was found in. I circled the room with the device, reaching as high as my arms would reach, covering every foot of each wall all the way to the floor. Once I finished that, I walked meticulously back and forth, doing a tic-tac-toe type of pattern in the room, holding the device at waist level. No anomalous readings were detected. I then repeated the pattern, holding the device approximately six inches off the floor. Nothing out of the ordinary was discovered with the EMF device.

I began to move to the next room. As I crossed the archway separating the two rooms, the device registered a 1.0, which is significant in this house. I stopped, dead in my tracks, to mark the spot where the device registered a fluctuation. There is no power turned on in the house, which makes it virtually impossible for the device to register a hit, or receive a false positive, due to the device picking up electrical bleed over. I slowly moved the device, first downwards, until the reading went to 0.0 milligauss. I then retraced my path, with the device, in an upwards direction, in an attempt to find out where the point of origin may be, that caused the device to register a reading. The higher I got, the higher the reading went. Once I reached approximately three inches from the bottom of the archway, the device registered a 2.9 on the milligauss scale and held steady from there to as close to the archway, as I could reach, without touching the device to the wood itself. What was blowing my mind, was the fact that this was the area where a man reportedly had hanged himself, in the house many years ago. To this point, there was no factual evidence supporting this rumor. I annotated the readings for later use and investigation.

I continued with my EMF sweep of the house. Moving through the archway and into the main room, which if you picture a cross in your mind, would be the center of the cross with each arm branching off from this center. There was a room to my left, a room directly in front of me, another room off to my right, and the long part of the cross was now behind me. I decided to check each room first and finish up with the center of the cross last.

Moving into the room on my left with the meter, I covered the entire room from top to bottom and the floor, with no positive readings whatsoever. As I began to exit the room, moving toward the room, that would be considered the top of the cross, I saw shadow movement off to my right. I stopped in my tracks, moving my head slowly to the right to get a better look at the area where I saw the movement. As my eyesight struggled to adjust to the darkness, after looking at the lights on the meter, I heard a little girl's voice say "Hi" right behind me. I nearly jumped out of my boots, as I was not expecting that at all. I stumbled forward, spinning around to try and see what had just said "Hi" to me, since I was the only person in the house as well as on the property. There was no one there. I quickly turned on my flashlight, scanning everything in sight, as I gathered myself from the jump-scare I had just received in the house. I replied, "Hi" as I scanned the room with my device, hoping for it to register a hit and give more validity that something was in the room with me. The device didn't reveal anything out of the ordinary. I told, whatever it was that said Hi to me, that it could touch the device and it would light up and it wouldn't hurt them.

I moved out of the room and toward the top of the cross room once again. This time I moved a little more slowly and deliberately in anticipation of something happening. Nothing did. I completed my sweep and to my surprise, nothing happened in this room with the meter nor were any disembodied voices heard. I now moved towards the last bedroom, the one with the notorious burn mark on the wall that resembles a goat head. This room is also, said to be, the location where the woman overdosed. The room itself had a very heavy, ominous feeling to it. As I moved into the room, I took my readings along the wall with the burn mark. Nothing registered as abnormal. I performed the sweep, as I had in all the other rooms up to this point. There was nothing irregular to report, other than, I couldn't help but notice, that the house seemed to have gotten even darker than it was when I started the sweep. I shook it off and went out of the room into the main area, that is the center of the cross. This is the area that many have said is the heart of the house. An area that seems to have a doorway between our world and the nether world.

As I moved into the room, I decided to move along the wall, that is essentially a circle, moving closer to the center of the room as I walked, almost in a whirlpool fashion. I moved around the circle slowly, making the circle smaller and smaller as I got to the very center of the room. I registered no fluctuation in the EMF, but as soon as I reached the center of the floor in the middle of the room, I felt a tremendous thump on the floor underneath me, that physically moved my feet under me, just a bit. I was startled, but not frightened out of my wits, because I had experienced this same situation, a couple of times, during previous investigations in the house. I stepped back and that's when the touch sensor on the Mel Meter went off, alerting me that it was maxed out.

It is important to explain how this function on the device works. There is a mini physical antenna, that can be extended out from the device. Once extended, you must press a button, on the back of the device, that says REM. This button turns on the REM function. When using this function on the device, there is an invisible area around the antenna, that when broken by something, physically severing the invisible field around the antenna, the device will sound alarms and lights. The closer to the antenna it is, the higher pitched the alarm is and the more lights are set off. For this device to be maxed out, something must be virtually touching the device or the antenna.

I felt that whatever had hit the floor underneath me, was the one and same thing that now had broken the plane of my device and was standing right in front of me. I was overcome with a dark negative feeling. I called out, "Do not touch me!" I decided now was a good time to take a break and regroup as I headed toward the kitchen, to the outside door. Just as I reached the kitchen door to head outside, I heard another loud bang, followed by a deep growling, gurgling sound, that came from somewhere close behind me. I wasted no time getting out of the house as I made a beeline for the garage.

I grabbed a drink from the cooler and went over to the seating area where there is: a small coffee table, a love seat, a La-Z-Boy chair, and two other chairs. Setting my gear down on the table, I flopped down into the chair. I exhaled a long, deep breath, attempting to slow my heart rate and to try to wrap my head around what I had just experienced, in the house, for the first time by myself. I knew three things: these spirits are intelligent, they are very interactive, and something in the house has reaffirmed for me, yet again ,that it is very negative in nature.

I also began to feel physically exhausted, beyond a normal range. All I wanted to do was to shut my eyes and take a nap. I, very quickly, fought this feeling off as I slammed down a caffeinated drink, stood up and began to pace back and forth in the garage. I did this for quite sometime, going back and forth in my mind, as to what my next step would be. I thought, on the one hand, I came here to investigate, and I will not let this negative spirit influence me. On the other hand, I thought maybe I should go to the hotel, get some rest and come back the next day, ready to go, full-bore, into it all day and night. After pondering this conundrum for quite a while, I decided I would go back in, do a couple of sessions, and call it a night.

I decided I would run a ghost box session. I began by grabbing a hack shack and standing in the dead center of the house. I started off by announcing out loud, "I am the new owner of this house! What do you think about that?" Immediately, a very deep growl seemed to come from the ghost box, followed by a female voice, telling me to leave. The tone, in the female voice, didn't feel as if it were making a threat, but rather it felt, almost like, she was trying to warn me. Just after, a distinct man's voice said, "Get out!" I got the overwhelming feeling, that it was the man who shot himself in the head, and he didn't want me in the house. I asked, "Why are you here?" and a fast response of "murder" came from the ghost box. I then said, "So you want to murder people, is that it?" A growling sound came from the box ,and that's when I felt as if something punched or stabbed me right in the stomach. I doubled over as the pain shot right through my body. As I was holding my stomach in pain, I called out, "Who just hit me in the stomach?" A growling, inaudible voice, that sounded like another language, emanated from the box. The word "energy" came out of the box. Still in a lot of pain, I managed to get another question out, saying, "Is this how you get your energy, by hurting people? Are you trying to take my energy?" A female voice answered, "Yes." I grabbed my cross on my neck and said, "Did you attack me because of my cross on my neck?" A bunch of growing and god-awful sounds emanated from the box, as if something was in pain from me pulling my cross out from under my shirt and showing it out in the open. I began to feel as if I was going to vomit, and I became very dizzy. I knew I had to stop the session. It was becoming more negative by the second. I felt as if I was about to pass out, and the last thing I wanted to do, was to pass out in that house, alone, with no help anywhere around. No one even knew I was there.

I stumbled my way through the house, out the door, and over to the garage, making my way to the couch. Just as I reached the couch, I saw tunnel vision and I must have blacked out, because I came to facedown on the couch. I don't think I was out for more than a few seconds, but I wasn't sure exactly how long, because I had lost track of time in all the commotion. I sat up on the couch and quickly noticed my stomach no longer hurt; the nausea and dizziness was gone.

I sat there stunned for more than an hour, running through it all in my head. Was the house testing me as the new owner? Were the negative spirits trying to kill me, or possess me? I had been to the house three prior times and it was never this bad. Was this some sort of dire warning? My head was spinning a million different ways. I knew only one thing at this point, I was done for the night.

I grabbed my gear, locked the doors to the house and garage, then headed for the hotel. Once I reached the four-lane highway, I mashed the pedal down on my Challenger and before I knew it, I was doing over 100 miles per hour. I was trying to put as much distance between the house and myself as possible. I got to the hotel at 2:30 a.m. I threw my luggage down on the desk, put the "Do not disturb" sign on the door, and fell onto the bed not even stopping to take my clothes off.

Day Two

I awoke and it was 2 p.m. the next day. I had slept more than 11 hours, and I felt like I had a hangover. My head was pounding, my body was as stiff as a board, and I was physically drained. I hadn't had a drop of anything to drink and I knew all to well what this was. It is what is referred to loosely, as a paranormal hangover. It happens when spirits attack you and attempt to drain your energy, for their own purposes, this is a common occurrence. I immediately went for my luggage and grabbed a pack of powdered vitamins, that I carry with me while investigating. I poured it in a bottle of water shook it up and slammed it down. I then slammed two more bottles of water without hesitation. I stripped off my clothes and headed for the shower. I grabbed a jug of kosher salt, poured some out in the hotel ice container, and took into the shower with me. Filling the container with water, I dumped it all over myself. I must have stayed in the shower for 45 minutes. I slowly recovered and headed out for some food. As I ate, I began to plan what I was going to do at the house that day. I decided I would set up my full-spectrum wireless DVR system in the garage, placing the four cameras, in various areas of the house, and record with them while I investigated. I would investigate outside, near the willow tree, and in the garage, finishing up inside the house.

I arrived at the house and went right to work, unloading the rest of my gear from the car and setting up the DVR system. The first camera, I would place in the crawl space under the house, facing the strange fire pit, that was put there, by God knows who and why. The second, I would place in the burn mark room, facing the burn mark, and the third would be in the room that the chair sits in. That camera would face the chair. The last camera, I would leave in the garage, facing my workstation. That way, if I was sitting there monitoring the cameras, I would be able to see if something was attempting to interact with me as well.

This night would be special, as I would have my friend Jeff Phillips in the house with me. Earlier in the evening, I had Jeff do an inspection of the house, just to get his impression of the construction of the house. Jeff, being in the insurance industry for more than 40 years, has been in thousands of structures, and what he relayed to me about the house was very telling. He stated that he had never seen any house built like this nor had he ever even heard of one being built like this one. You can read his thoughts about the house later in the book.

Jeff, being a paranormal guy himself, would stick around and investigate the house with me as well. I gave Jeff the hack shack ghost box and had him stand in the dead center of the house. When the box was turned on, immediately there was a growling sound coming out of it. This sound was of such a nature, that I had never heard this sound come out of that particular box, ever, and I have owned it for more than 12 years. It had me very perplexed and still does to this day. We began to ask questions and I saw a strange white light manifest out of thin air and move from left to right, for about two feet ,and then disappear. I said out loud, "Who just showed themselves to us? Who's in here with us?" Just then a voice said, "Baal or Bael." According to Christian lore, this demon is said to be Satan's assistant, and commands 66 legions of demons. Some demonologists say that his power is greater during the month of October and that the origins of

Halloween, in Samhain, began with pagan rituals conducting sacrifices as well as worshipping this demon. Was it coincidence that it was the month of October, during the week of Halloween, and we were getting this name coming from the hack shack? I'm not so sure. I asked out loud, "Who just said that demonic name?" and a female voice came out of the box and said, "me." I ran with it and asked, "Did you conjure anything into this house?" A voice quickly answered with the word, "devil." It was getting very heavy in the house very quickly. But we pushed on, as we heard insect-type noises coming out of the box now. Jeff reported feeling dizzy and a bit disoriented at this time. We asked several other questions with no audible or clear responses.

I decided to go and retrieve another box from the garage while Jeff conducted an EVP session. He was now alone in the house. He reported hearing a very faint female moaning sound and a very loud thump that seemed to have originated from under the floor of the house, a common occurrence, reported by many people who have spent time in the house. Still feeling a bit woozy, Jeff moved into the room where one of the double doors is said to have been shattered by an unseen force, slamming it violently on one occasion. He sat on the couch using the ghost box, while I filmed the session. He asked who had slammed the doors in this room, when a deep, growly voice said with authority, "LEAVE!" At that exact moment, two strange light anomalies manifested, one after the other; one for a few seconds and then each disappeared. Then the word "hung" came out of the box. Was this a reference to the young man who hung himself in the archway of the house? The word "demon," followed by "rape" came out of the box next. I asked, "Is there an incubus or succubus in the house?" Immediately, the response was "incubus." We were getting very clear and intelligent communication, with something in the house, and it was so heavy and thick in the house, it was becoming hard to breath.

The box said "Jeff," as to call him out and let him know it knew his name. It then said, "Shadow" followed by a loud, guttural growl. He asked, "Who is the shadow?" The same female voice from the start of the session replied, "Me." I followed up with, "What entity controls this house?" A very quick male voice responded, "Baal" for the second time, referencing the same demon name, that was said at the beginning of our night in the house. I asked, "Were you conjured here?" The same male voice said, "Yes," "Spirit." It was becoming clearer, that there most likely, was some sort of witchcraft, that may have been conducted in this house, during its long history.

As all of this was going on, I had people who were watching the DVR system live. They were typing in the live chat room, saying that they were seeing something moving behind me, as Jeff said the same thing, at the exact same. The energy was getting very chaotic all around us now. The word "gun" came from the ghost box. I immediately asked, "Whoever said that, what is your name?" The same voice replied the name of the man who shot himself. It was astonishing to get the name of the man who shot himself. Continuing with the ghost box session, the next random word that came from the box was Jeff,. Asking out loud "Who said that name?" The same voice said, "shadow." The spirit box was spitting out so many relevant responses, it was mind-blowing. In fact, the responses were so fast and so many, that it was difficult to keep up. A startling phrase that came from the box said, "There's blood here." Knowing the house's history, the number of deaths, and the manner of deaths, this phrase was spot on.

As the night went on, the amount of responses began to dwindle down. I decided to call it a night around 4 a.m. I was feeling completely drained and my defenses were becoming weaker. I knew it was time to get out of house before something bad happened. Jeff had left about two hours prior, due to having another engagement early the next day. Being in the Weep is dangerous enough. Being there alone is recipe for disaster. I locked up the house, packed up my gear, and headed up the road to the hotel.

Day Three

I woke up around 3 p.m. again feeling hung over. I rolled over, reaching the nightstand for a bottle of water, that I had pre-positioned there, the night before. I twisted the lid off and slammed the entire bottle down. I lay there in the bed for another twenty minutes, trying to pull myself together enough to sit up. Still feeling as dry as the desert, I sat up in the bed and grabbed a second bottle of water and began to slam it down as if I hadn't drunk water in a week. Once finished, I summoned all the energy I could and hobbled over to the bathroom. I cranked the shower on, climbed in and, under the icy water, attempted to wake myself up. It was pure misery as the cold water ran over my head and down my body, but the desired effect was achieved. In no time, I felt alive once again. Once I finished my shower, I headed over to grab yet another bottle of water. This time I added my favorite concoction to the water; a powdered vitamin pack. I slammed it down as I got dressed and headed out for breakfast. I took my time eating as I contemplated my plan of action, for the third night at the house. Darkness was fast approaching as I headed down the road for the 30-minute drive to the house. On my way there, I decided I had enough time to stop at the graveyard where the man who shot himself was buried.

When I arrived at the site, it was about an hour before dark and I had to get a move on to get set up. I grabbed my go bag with my equipment. It held a camera, a ghost box, a digital recorder and an EMF meter. Once I reached the headstone, I placed the EMF meter on the top of it and turned it on. I set my camera, on a tripod, facing the headstone and I grabbed the digital recorder. As I began the EVP session, it was eerily quiet and there were no living souls in sight anywhere. I started by speaking to him directly. I explained that I was now the new owner of the house and I meant no disrespect. All I wanted to do was make contact with him, if he was here, and to know if there was something bad in the house that had coerced him, or took control over him in some way, that may have influenced him into committing suicide. I told him that he could speak into the orange light on the recorder and I would be able to play it back to hear his responses. I told him, he would also be able to hear his own voice upon playback. I said if you understand what I just said, you can touch this device to confirm to me you understand —I was referring to the EMF meter. I watched the meter for approximately 30 seconds but nothing happened. I then proceeded with the EVP session.

The first question I asked was, "Are you here with me now? The second question I asked was, "Is there something negative or evil in nature in your old house?" The third question I asked was, "Did something in the house make you commit suicide?" I played the recorder back and listened intently for a response. There was no response to the first three questions. I decided to ask the same three questions once again. I asked the first two and had just finished asking the third question again, when the EMF meter lit up like a Christmas tree. It was maxed out on the touch sensor and audible alarm system. This startled me a bit and I jumped back a couple of steps. I quickly stopped the recorder and played it back. There was no response to the first two questions, but after the third question of me asking, "Did something in the house cause you to commit suicide?" there was a very low but distinct, drawn out "Yes!" This blew me away because I got the response of "Yes" on the recorder and the meter had gone off at the same time. A horrible feeling came over me and I got the cold chills, from my head to my toes as the energy seemed to change, very quickly, to an ominous feeling all around me. It was also becoming darker by the minute. I wanted more information, to try and confirm, if it was in fact, the spirit of the man that I was communicating with in the cemetery. I asked several times, "If that was you, do something right now, to confirm with me, that it was you who answered the question. Make the meter go off again, make a sound, say your name on the recorder when I count to three." I began to count: 1, 2, 3. "Do it now," I called out loud. I waited for several seconds, then I played the recorder back and listened intently, hearing no response. I was disappointed, but I never gave up.

I asked again and again for him to let me know it was him, but nothing happened. Then it dawned on me, as it was now too dark to see, that perhaps it wasn't him, but something else — something very bad in nature that had responded to my question. Again, the cold chills ran the length of my entire body. I decided I had better pack up and head to the house. I quickly retrieved my flashlight from my pack and turned it on, as I packed my gear up, placing it into the bag. I hightailed it from the graveyard, out to my car and down the road I went.

On my way to the house, I began to feel very weak and nauseated. It was only about seven miles to the house from the graveyard, but this sick feeling was getting worse by the second. I reached a gas station, went straight into the bathroom and started throwing cold water on my face. It didn't matter. I began to throw up violently in the toilet. After several goes at it, I stopped the vomiting. I again threw cold water on my face and cleaned myself up a bit. I knew then, whatever it was I had communicated with, was pissed I was there, trying to talk with the man who shot himself, in an attempt to garner information as to what lurks in the house.

I knew my defenses were down already from my energy being drained at the house, so I had to make a call, and the call was to take the night off from investigating the house. Everything in me was telling me to go investigate the house, but I had to ask myself, "Was this a trap?" Was this dark entity laying a trap for me so it could attack me even further? I decided it was not worth the risk and I headed back to the hotel. Once I got to the hotel, I drew a bath and poured kosher salt in the water. I jumped in and soaked for an hour in order to cleanse myself of the negative energy. After I finished my bath, I ordered a pizza in. I decided to clear my head by watching a movie for the night, trying not to focus on the house in any way. I ate my pizza and enjoyed a couple of movies before I succumbed to Mr. Sandman.

Day 4

I awoke at noon feeling refreshed and full of energy. The kosher salt bath seemed to have done the trick. I headed to the restaurant to grab some food and prepare for the night's investigation.

I arrived at the house, went straight in and conducted a spirit box session using the SB-7 Spirit box. I stood in the very center of the house, where I believe there is a doorway, a portal if you will, to the other side. I talked out loud, as if someone else was in the room with me. I asked the spirits or entities, that reside in the house, to talk with me and reveal themselves in any way they chose, except they could not use my energy to do so. I explained that they could use any of the devices that I had in the room to communicate with me. I used a firm and direct tone of voice, hoping this would elicit some sort of response to my questions.

I turned on the SB-7 and the first thing that came out of it was, "I know you!" This was compelling, as I thought to myself, "What or who in the hell is telling me they know me?" I followed up by saying, "Who knows me?" No response. I asked again, "You say you know me. I'd like to know who you are." No response. I asked one more time, "Who said they know me?" Again, no response. This got under my skin a bit, so I called it out and said, "You're full of it. You don't know me!" Just then, a sinister giggle came out of the SB-7. Of course, I became even more agitated and I responded by saying, "Oh you think this is funny, do you?" No response. I realized that it was already trying to manipulate me. I immediately went into a different line of questioning. I asked, "Why was this house built in the shape it is?" Immediately, a darker and deeper, sinister giggle came out of the spirit box. It was getting very intense already and I hadn't been in the house ten minutes.

I continued asking, "Was this house built for witchcraft practices?" Again the evil giggle emanated out of the box. I asked, "What's under our feet right now?" Again the giggle, then a woman's voice answered, "A pit," This was insane because there is a strange pit, that was dug into the dirt of the crawl space and has granite rocks surrounding it, much like a fire pit you would build if you were camping. It also has ash in the bottom of it. The strange dark laughing and giggling were coming out of the box repeatedly now; in fact, so much so that I couldn't get a question in. It was purposely toying with my emotions trying to get under my skin.

I tried my best to ignore the laughing and move forward with my questions, as the laughing was now non-stop. I said, "You know I'm close to finding something out, don't you?" Immediately, a laugh again. Just then I felt something touch my face. I shouted out, "DO NOT TOUCH ME!" I knew it was trying to attack me at this point. The laughing came again, but even more sinister and pronounced in nature. In all my years of investigating the paranormal, I had never experienced such a mocking. Something was trying its hardest to manipulate me into anger. Luckily, I had realized this fairly quickly and wasn't about to play into its game. Often, negative entities will try and manipulate your emotions, to gain access to your psyche, and feed off your energy. I was not going to allow this to happen. I felt as if I was in an emotional war to fend this thing off.

I repeated the question, "What is under this house?" A response of "Leave" came out of the box. It appeared that I may have turned the tide and now I was annoying it. I posed the question once again, "What is under this house?" The response was "Blood." This time, the answer came from a very familiar, male voice, I had heard numerous times in the house, over several different investigations. Could this be the man who shot himself, pushing his way forward, trying to give me information? Perhaps. The only thing I could do was keep pressing forward by asking more questions.

I stepped over to the room where the woman who overdosed was said to have died, and I asked, "Who died in this room over here?" The name of the man, who shot himself, came out of the spirit box. Was this misinformation or was the information I had wrong? Was the spirit I was communicating with trying to give me false information or true information? At this point anything was possible. An unprovoked word came out of the box, "Death." Again, this was very intelligent and factual information. This house has had many deaths in it. Even though I love those kinds of responses, when investigating, it becomes very frustrating at times, to get the information you are seeking, when conducting these sessions, after many hours.

Other unprovoked words began to come from the box: "Demon," followed by "Here." That's when I saw a very dark shadow figure, in the front room of the house, going from left to right. Then the REM Pod went off as if something was touching it. The energy was very fast and furious now and gaining momentum. I said, "Are you trying to sneak around behind me now?" Again, the evil giggling laugh came from the box. I looked at my watch and was stunned to discover that an hour and a half had gone by. It had felt like only few minutes. Had this entity been manipulating the time or even my sense of time at this point? That's when my name came out of the box, "Dave" followed by several growls and grunt sounds.

I began to realize how out of sorts I was. It was almost as if I was in some sort of dream state now. My sense of time was totally gone. Everything felt different, like I was in another world, not the world as we know it but in their world. I felt out of control, like everything was spinning around and I was on the inside looking out into our world. It was time to get the hell out of there and fast. I quickly turned off the spirit box, grabbed my camera and left the house. As soon as I was out of the house and took my first breath of fresh air, everything snapped back to normal. Nothing felt distorted any longer. I quickly noticed that my head was pounding, as if someone was hitting me in the forehead with a mini sledgehammer, as every beat of my heart became more agonizing. I don't ever recall having such a severe headache in my life.

I made my way over to the garage where I had my makeshift control center set up, grabbed a bottle of ibuprofen and struggled getting the lid off. I remember dumping several of the pills in my hand and throwing them in my mouth, followed by gulping down half a bottle of water to wash them down. I knew I had to leave the property and fast. I grabbed my keys and jogged to my vehicle. I jumped in and sped off away from the house as quickly as I could. The farther I got away, the quicker my headache seemed to go away. I felt as if I just escaped from something. What it was I'm still not sure, but to this day I know it was very bad. It appeared to me that I had angered something, and it was letting me know it.

CHAPTER 10
ALL HALLOWS EVE 2017

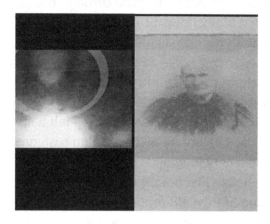

Apparition on Left Mary Ann Sykes on Right
Photo Credit: Living Dead Paranormal

Day 5

After a hair-raising experience on night four, I was feeling a bit apprehensive about going back to the house for night five, especially on All Hallows' Eve. After all, it is said that the veil between the world of the living and the world of the dead is most thin on this night. I knew I had to push through any fears I may have, in order to document any further phenomena that might take place at the house. There were a few things that I still wanted to do at the house, the first being lighting up a large bonfire in the backyard. Both Brenda and the groundskeeper had told me that, in previous years, anytime they had a big fire in the backyard, the spirit activity had increased significantly in the house. I wanted to test this theory and take it a bit farther by doing it on All Hallows' Eve. It made perfect sense, that if it was true about what Brenda and Rocky had told me occurred when fires were lit on the property, and the veil being the thinnest between the world of the living and the world of the dead, this would be a perfect opportunity to test the theory out.

I would also investigate the crawl space under the house this night, where the strange fire pit is located and the child's arm bone was found by Rocky. I kept thinking about what I had gone through the night before in the house, and after giving it many hours of thought in the hotel room, I decided that I would continue with my investigation.

The final day began much like all the others. I woke up feeling like I had been on a long night of drinking and fighting. My body, mind, and soul were extremely tired. I stumbled my way into the bathroom and cleansed myself with kosher salt and after quite some time I felt halfway human once again. I headed out for a very late meal. I was in no rush on this day to get to the house. I knew I had a very long night ahead of me.

I arrived at the house just before dark. I decided to head into the garage and review some of the DVR footage, from the time I left. I wanted to see if anything noticeable had occurred while I was away and also just to kind of ease into the night's investigation. After skimming through the footage for more than an hour, I didn't notice anything that jumped out and grabbed me, so I decided to go outside and start the bonfire up. As I walked around the fire pit, an overwhelming feeling of being watched came over me. I quickly looked back behind me and that's when I noticed it was a straight shot from the second story window directly overlooking the fire pit. As I stared at the window for several seconds, feeling as if something was watching me from inside the house, I saw movement in the window and the cold chills went all through my body. As I shivered, I realized that had been where the feeling was coming from. I had just experienced what Brenda, and so many others in her family, had experienced so many other times; being watched by something non-living from within the house.

I wanted the fire to get started fast. I took some of the gas and oil mix, I had at the house for my chainsaw, and threw it on the nearly six-foot-high stack of tree limbs and wood that had been placed in the massive fire pit behind the barn. I lit up a wad of newspaper and threw it in. The fire burst to life, with a massive whoosh sound, as it quickly spread about the dry limbs. In no time at all I had a 20-foot-high wall of flame going. I headed back in to grab my hack shack and camera to conduct a fire ITC session in the backyard.

I returned to the fire pit and the fire was still blazing hot with massive eight-foot-high flames. I cranked the hack shack on and let it run, listening intently for any relevant information to come through. At the same time, I walked around the fire, with a full-spectrum camera, filming the flames to see if I could capture anything trying to manifest in the flames. I started out by saying out loud "If there are any spirits that reside in the house or on the property that wish to speak or show themselves in the fire, feel free." I turned on the hack shack spirit box to see if anything decides to be heard. Immediately a voice says, "Hot, dirty, beware, and G-d dammit!" followed by the name "Edward" and the word "Rape." All of this happened before I could even ask a question.

My first question was, "Are you trying to show yourself in the fire?" A woman's voice answered immediately saying, "Yes." A man's voice came across and said the name "Michael," followed by "St. Michael." Then a woman's voice said, "Leave." Then I asked, "What's that called in front of me?" referring to the fire. A male voice said, "Devil." I quickly asked, "Is something evil coming through the fire?" A response in a female voice said, "Witch," followed by "Dragon." It was getting very interesting to say the least, as I had heard many similar responses, in the house, on many occasions before the investigation tonight. I couldn't help but wonder, if the fire that was burning right in front of me, was possibly giving any of the negative entities, that reside on the property more energy. I asked if the fire was giving them more power, and a voice responded, "Fuck Dave."

This kind of response is what I look for while investigating. Although it is extremely negative in nature and directed specifically towards me, it shows that the spirit box does indeed work for several reasons. First it proves it is not radio bleed over due to the fact that it is against FCC regulations for curse words to be used on the radio. Second, the statement was directed towards me specifically and I know this to be fact, simply because my real name is David, however I go by Dave in most cases. This spirit or entity, that addressed me, used my nickname cursing me. There is no coincidence in that whatsoever in my opinion. I continued the fire ITC session for approximately 45 minutes, as the fire burned down lower and lower. And it was uncanny, as the fire got weaker, the responses also seemed to diminish in frequency and accuracy.

The last significant responses that were received were after the word "Shadow" came from the box. I asked, "Who's the shadow?" A clear response of, "Spirit" in a man's voice, came out of the box. But what really unnerved me was when a woman's voice came from the box, I'll never forget this, it said, "Dave's mother." I quickly responded "No, you're not going there." My mother had been dead since 1992, and I knew this was a ploy by a negative entity to gain access to me, by using the pain and sadness over the loss of my mother. This was not the first instance that something negative, had tried to use the death of my mom, to slip in and try and gain access through a tragic event that transpired in my life. Often times these negatives, will try and gain your trust, by acting as if they are a dead loved one wanting to communicate with you. They also may try acting as if they are a small child, often a little girl, to make you feel sorry for them. In my opinion, it is all a ploy, in a sadistic attempt to ultimately find a way into your psyche, with the ultimate goal of possessing you or attaching itself to you. I ended the session immediately and returned to the control center for a break before I was to enter the house and continue the investigation into Halloween.

The next part of the investigation was to become, one of the craziest things I had ever attempted, during an investigation. I would crawl under the house, where Rocky was attacked by an unseen force, just after he accidentally uncovered a child's arm bone in a mound of dirt under there. The crawl space also contains a mysterious fire pit, that still holds ash in it to this day and no one seems to know why it's there or who put it there. I had taken a good 30-minute break since the fire ITC session. I drank a couple of bottles of water, saged myself, and I felt rejuvenated enough to attempt the next session under the house. As far as I knew, no one had ever attempted this at the house. I needed some answers as to what may have occurred under this house. I also needed to see the pit and the mounds of dirt for myself at this point. Up until now, I had only ventured a few feet into the crawl space, to place a static DVR camera under the house. I knew it wasn't going to be pleasant under there. It was a small, cramped space, that a big guy like me would have problems moving around in. I would have to crawl on my belly, most of the way in, to keep from scraping my back or banging my head off of the floor joists.

I made my way to the door in the floor, that leads to the crawl space and removed it. I got down in the hole and, squatting down as I reached for my camera, pulled it down with me, being careful not to knock it around too much. Getting on all fours, I slowly and carefully made my way into the tight, small space, passing by my static camera I had placed there five days earlier. The area slowly began to open up as I made my way past the camera, and I was able to crawl on my hands and knees without much extra effort. However, it was cumbersome trying to bring the camera rig along for the trip. I would push it forward, a foot or two, and then catch up to it, push it forward then crawl to it; a very slow and tedious process but a necessary one.

I began to look for the fire pit but saw nothing, until I came upon a support stack of bricks located nearly in the center of the house. Once I got my head just past this support column, there it was just past the column. An approximately two- to three-foot-wide hole in the ground, surrounded by what appeared to be granite rocks. I crawled to the edge so I could see into the hole, and sure enough there appeared to be ash in the bottom of the hole. The hole itself was about a foot and a half deep. I was very skeptical when I first heard about the fire pit story, but I knew now it did exist.

I crawled about five more feet past the pit, to where I figured the dead center of the house was. I shined my flashlight around the crawl space, trying to get my bearings. Off to my right, I noticed the several mounds of dirt, where Rocky had said he came across the arm bone of the child. I realized I was in the thick of it, and this was as good of a place as any to conduct a session. I positioned my camera facing me, and I set up a Mel Meter, a ghost box and a digital recorder next to the camera. My knees and back were already killing me. I decided that lying down would be the most comfortable position to conduct the session. I was just about to start when I heard, what sounded like footsteps above me, coming from inside the house. I froze, holding my breath, as I listened to the footsteps pass directly over my head, walking towards the main room of the house. I listened intently, knowing there was no living person in the house. I suddenly realized someone, or something was in the house, right above my head and I was there alone. Once the footsteps went past me, they became less pronounced and seemed to fade away.

I turned on the hack shack ghost box and asked, "How many are buried down here?" A female responded, "Many." My next question was, "Are they all children?" The response by the same woman's voice said, "Four." The next thing that happened, blew my mind. A man's voice said, "Girl, five." Was this spirit talking about the child's arm bone that was found under the house? Was he saying it belonged to a little girl who was five years old when she died, or was he trying to tell me there were five different girls buried under the house? I wasn't sure, but either way you go with it, it's downright horrifying.

The air under the house was very heavy and it felt extremely negative, like something was down there with me, watching me, waiting to attack me at any moment. I still wanted to communicate, but I had to overcome the fear of not being able to move and see in all directions around me, while under the house. Because of this overwhelming feeling, of something not wanting me down there, I asked out loud, "Does something not want me down here?" The response was, "Beast." It was becoming clearer, this just might be the entry point, or even the lair of the negative entity that resides in the house.

Just to get confirmation, I asked the spirit box, if there were bodies buried down here. The response came quickly and very clearly, "Yeah." I began to see shadow movement all around me, darting around, just out of range of the Infrared lights on the camera. I grabbed my regular flashlight and began lighting up the entire crawl space, trying to see if I could make out anything that might be moving around under the house with me. In each area I shone the light, there was nothing there. I heard the sound of, something, shuffling in the dirt behind me. I quickly rolled from my side onto my back and hit that area with my flashlight. There was nothing there. All of a sudden, the same shuffling, was now behind me in the other direction. I rolled up onto my side again, shooting the flashlight in that direction, and again nothing was there. Again, I heard the sound behind me, toward the direction where my feet were. I rolled onto my back once again, with the light pointing in that direction, and nothing was there again.

My heart was pumping pretty hard now, as I realized something was under there with me, playing games, trying to strike fear into me and use that to weaken me. I rolled onto my stomach and resumed asking questions, I said, "You like to play games, don't you?" An evil-sounding laugh came out of the box, and then I heard the shuffling sound toward my feet again. I rolled back over with the light yet again, shinning in that direction, seeing nothing. I closed my eyes for a few seconds and recited the Lord's Prayer. I did this in order to regain my composure and to protect myself from the negative spirit, or entity, that was trying to cause havoc with me. Once I was done, I felt relieved and reinvigorated to continue on with the session.

My head began to get an extreme headache, which in this house was a sign that something was trying to affect me physically again. I refocused back to the strange fire pit under the house and I asked if it was used in rituals. A response of "Yeah" came out of the box in a man's voice. Then a very clear "Get out" came out of the box followed by my name, "Dave." It was still very negative under the house and was getting worse as time went by. Out of nowhere I felt as if something grabbed my foot. I quickly yanked my leg away saying, "Don't freaking touch me." I quickly changed the subject, asking, "Who or what attacked Rocky down here?" A woman's voice responded, "Dark spirit." This was an amazing response, as Rocky himself told me how evil it felt to him when he was attacked. At this moment, I observed a dark shadow, pass by the little window, to the outside of the crawl space. My whole body was feeling a static charge, as it again felt as if something was grabbing my foot. I leaned up on my elbows with my flashlight and saw nothing in that direction. I called out loud not to touch me. The word "Demon" came out of the box followed by "Assault." The feeling began to get even more intense down there, and I felt as if any minute, I would be severely attacked. I asked, "Is there evil that lurks under this house?" The response was "Total," followed by a whole flurry of demonic-sounding growls, hisses, and screams. The words "Possessed" and "Cursed" came out of the box next and I asked, "Were the people who killed themselves in the house possessed?" The response was unreal. A woman's voice, said the name of the man, who shot himself. We know that the last man who lived in the house, had shot himself in the head and died in the house. Therefore, it makes perfect sense, that if there is a negative force or presence in the house or on the property, it may in fact have influenced people, who had spent any significant time in the house, to hurt themselves in some way. We know this to be prevalent, in many negative haunting cases, worldwide. In many of these instances, people who have encountered a negative presence for long periods of time, either have hurt people close to them or even committed suicide in some cases.

The more answers I was getting, the more it felt as if something was trying to affect me negatively. My headache was getting worse, and my energy level was diminishing very quickly again, as words like "Attack" and "Kill" began to pour out of the spirit box, at a staggering rate. I asked, "Where do you come from? " Two distinct responses came out of the box. The first was, "Hell, " followed by "Earth" in a male voice, then a different voice said, "Get out."

Again, I noticed, what appeared to be, at least three different shadows moving around at the edge of where my visual sight could recognize. I sat up to get a better look, when four distinct voices saying "Help" came from the spirit box. There was a flurry of swirling energy down there with me, coming from many different sources. At this point, it was getting very confusing, trying to figure out what was happening. It was as if I were standing in a crowd of people and all of them were trying to talk to me at once; and in that crowd of people, there were several hiding behind the others, waiting to attack me at any moment. That's when I saw a pair of yellow eyes, peering at me from behind one of the support pillars, at the far front corner of the house.

As soon as I noticed them, the word "yellow" came out of the spirit box. I pointed my light toward that direction and saw nothing else. I turned it off and still nothing there. The cold chills coursed through my body, at the mere thought of what was behind those yellow eyes. I grabbed my holy water out of my pocket, poured it all over myself and decided to end my time under the house. But before I did, I asked one last question, "Is the creature, with the yellow eyes, what affected me last night? " A clear female voice responded, "Yes." That was all I needed to hear. My energy was nearly completely depleted, and I knew I still had to pack up all my gear. I still had a long night ahead of me. As I prepared my gear, to make the crawl out of the hole under the house, I was about to turn off the spirit box, when a growly man's voice said very adamantly and defiantly, "I WANT YOU TO LEAVE!" That was enough for me for the night. It was time to make the crawl out of there, before something bad happened.

I began to crawl out of the hole under the house, when I heard a distinct growl and hiss, as if something was behind me. I crawled as fast as I could, finally reaching the entrance to the crawl space. Up and out I went, feeling as if something was right behind me. I pulled myself out of there, grabbing the board that covered the hole and slamming it down over the entrance. I grabbed my camera and gear as I headed for my control center, feeling relieved for the moment.

I packed my gear in record time. All I could think about was getting the hell out of there and away from the property. I don't ever recall having such a strong feeling to leave; it was overwhelming. After loading all my gear and locking up the house, I covered my car, gear, and lastly myself with holy water. I said a prayer for nothing to follow me, jumped in my car and headed down the road toward the hotel.

Feeling exhausted once I reached my hotel room, I stripped off my clothes and jumped in the shower. I wanted to just relax in the hotel, watch TV for a bit and not spend one-second thinking about the house and the week-long investigation I just did. Just as I got comfortable on my bed, I heard the distinct sound of a light switch clicking and the fan in the bathroom came on. I jumped up and ran to the bathroom and, sure enough, the bathroom fan was on. Since I was the only one in the room, I wondered how this could have happened. At first. I thought that maybe the switch was fouled up, was stuck in the middle between on and off and it just clicked on by itself. I tested this theory, trying to purposely make the switch stay in the middle, between off and on. No matter how many times I tried to make it do this, it would not stay stuck in the middle. It was either in the off or on position. I backed up, standing there looking at the switch, puzzled. Then I noticed the giant mirror on the wall, right next to the bathroom entrance. Could it have been, that something followed me back through the mirror at the house, and the mirror in my hotel room? There is a long-standing theory, that mirrors, are and can be used as a doorway for spirits to travel through. I can't say that's what happened for sure, but it sure did feel like a possibility at the time. I covered the mirrors up with towels, and shook holy water all over my room, hoping this would keep anything else from attempting to follow me home.

It had been an entire year and a half since I'd been back to the house I own. What I experienced during that week, has affected me like no other location I have ever investigated before. During that year and half, I had been approached by many people asking to investigate the notorious Willows Weep house. Many are wiling to pay for their time there. However, after experiencing what I did there, I wasn't so sure I would let just anyone investigate the house, primarily because the house, in my opinion and several others' opinions, is just too negative in nature.

After talking to several of my colleagues in the field about this, I decided, for the time being, I would allow only seasoned investigators into the house, people I know who can: recognize when they are being affected by something negative; who know when it is time to pull the plug and get out of there when necessary. That way, I will see what they feel is going in the house too. We can compare notes, experiences and any evidence captured in the house or on the property. Since that time, only a handful of experienced investigators, have been allowed inside the house known as Willows Weep, and their experiences and evidence captures have been very eye-opening to say the least. In general, most of them agree with me that the Weep is very negative in nature; so much so that they believe novice investigators should not be allowed inside the structure. However, I bought the house, for it to be a location for all to study paranormal phenomena and, at some point, I feel I will open it back up for the general public to investigate it once, I feel, the time is right.

I returned to the house in February 2019, but it was not to conduct your typical paranormal investigation. It was to film an episode for a new TV show called "The UnXplained" on the History channel. I had been approached, in January 2019, about putting the house on an episode called Evil Places. I agreed to do it because, having investigated so many locations over the years, none of them even comes close to the history of this house and all the paranormal factors that are associated with it. I feel that it deserves to be brought to light -- the history of this house and the area around it. With that being said, there is much more to be discovered about this property and the people who lived there. We often leave these locations with more questions than answers, and even though I feel that I, and several other investigators, have made progress in getting closer to some answers as to what forces are lurking within the walls of this house, essentially many new questions have come to the forefront as a result of these investigations. I often stop and wonder if, since I am the new owner, will I be attacked violently like Brenda and members of her family were? Will I become the new target of the negative force that seems to thrive off of hurting people, causing them to commit suicide? The only logical answer to that would be time itself.

The one thing we can do, as investigators of the strange and unknown, is try and document phenomena as it occurs. We can dig deep into the history of the land, the people, and what may have transpired at any given location. We use various theories and investigation techniques in order to garner some type of interaction, from a deceased person or no human entity, all in the hopes of getting a small piece, to a much bigger puzzle. It is my hope that using this location as a paranormal lab, can somehow further the field of the paranormal by developing new investigation techniques, plus new ways of communicating with these spirits and entities. Currently, there are several ongoing projects being conducted on-site. One thing is for sure, this is only the tip of the iceberg when it comes to the house that sits in the tiny town of Cayuga, Indiana. In my opinion and numerous other investigators' opinions, there is something very negative and malevolent, that has either been conjured there or has been there for thousands of years before us.

CHAPTER 11

NightStalkers™
PARANORMAL RESEARCH

BARRY GAUNT

I've known Barry Gaunt for a few years now, but have known of him much longer. He is also known as the "Kentucky Truth Seeker." "Bear," as his friends call him, is a very well-known investigator throughout many circles in the paranormal. He investigates all aspects of unexplained phenomena. His reputation as a methodical investigator precedes him. It was an honor to have him investigate the house with his team. He is another one that will tell it like it is, when it comes to what he believes about any given location. As with most Investigators, his reputation means everything to him, and he would never say a location is experiencing unexplained happenings if it were not true. It was an honor to have him put his expertise to use at Willows Weep. The following report and eyewitness accounts are from his and his team's first investigation at the house.

Form 7 - Members Investigation Log
Location Information:

Investigator:	Barry "Bear" Gaunt	Date:	8/14/2018	Time:	6:45PM-EST	to	3:00AM-EST

Location:	Willows Weep, 5173 N. Elm Tree Rd. Cayuga IN. 47928 (Known Haunted Home, Owner: Dave Spinks)

Type of Structure: Residential Commercial   Historical   Abandoned
Cemetery   Other - If Other, explain:

Residential with outbuildings (2) Historical, abandoned (No one lives in the home)

Rooms Investigated:	Barn (Garage), All Interior rooms of Home (including both Bathrooms) CTV Camera 4 in home, 1 additional CTV was used to monitor the crawl space under the home. Home had no power used 3500watt generator for power, (1) laptop and Verizon internet link 4K system.

realsupernatural202@gmail.com

Weather:	Avg temp that night 71 degrees, Fair conditions	Moon Phase:	Waxing Crescent

Other Investigators Present:	Melvin Brazzle and Steve Miller

Equipment Used:

Std. Digital Camera	NV Digital Camera	Digital Audio Recorder	# of IR Motion Sensors:	(2)
IR Thermometer	Digital Thermometer	Analog Thermometer	Other Weather Device:	Weather Underground
EMF Meter	K-II Meter	Mel Meter	Geophone	
DVR System	# of cameras:	Locations:		

(3)-Std. Digital Camera, Full Spectrum NV Digital Camera, (5) Digital Recorders, (2) IR Thermometer, (2) EMF Meters,

(2) K-II Meters, (1) Mel Meter with ADS & REM Pod, (1) Rem Pod, (1) Geophone, (5) DVR NV IR Cameras

(2) Handheld Digital Camcorder:	HDD	Tapes (# used)	Tape Length:	DVD
Static/Tripod (Y)	NV (Y)	External Illuminators (# and type)	(5) 900 TVL Wide Angle IR NV to 90ft	
Other:	(3) Hand held IR Illuminators and (2) Hand held Full Spectrum Illuminators.			

Phenomena as witnessed by Barry Gaunt

Time 7:15 p.m.

After meeting Rocky and taking a quick guided tour of the home. I Installed (2) new AA batteries in Zoom 5 Recorder. I placed it on coffee table, in main room, on a small static tri-pod,. The home was empty and had no power. No Investigators were in the home, because we all were outside setting up a generator and the command center in the garage/barn including the DVR system. We came back into the home, to set up static cameras to DVR, and I noticed that the lights were out on my Zoom 5 recorder. It was totally dead. I picked up the recorder and removed it from the home. I took it to the command center and installed two new AA batteries. I did not set it back up, in the home, during the rest of the cameras set up. After the investigation, while reviewing the evidence back at my home, I was shocked to find, that during the set-up time, the recorder was in the house, it ran for only 18 mins before batteries were totally drained. The amazing part was that the recorder captured 36 EVPs during that time. Which means there was an EVP captured, every 30 seconds, during the recorder run time!

Time 9 p.m. – I was going to broadcast live from the home on the radio show. I was set up in the command center in the garage/barn. After starting show, odd sounds and other oddities happen on my end, seemed liked something or someone was interfering with the equipment. I lost all power to the computer and internet device Without power to these devices, I was unable to broadcast but my cohost did continue the radio show without me. At around 10:35 p.m., all investigators were taking a break, in the garage/barn. I was sitting in front of the computer and it came on by itself! The radio show's page came up and internet was on! The show ends at 10:30. When my laptop restarted, it should have gone into facial recognition and a manual 2nd password must be entered to bring up my desktop, none of this happened. I cannot explain how this happened!!!

Time 11 p.m.

All investigators entered the home. As we were standing in suicide room, preparing to do a ghost box session, I set my record down and it fell on the floor. Right after this, one of the fishing poles on the wall fell on the floor. No one was within 3ft from it, and it was not touched by any investigators to our knowledge.

Time 11:12 p.m.

I said, "My name is Bear. Have you heard of me?" We heard what sounded like a disembodied voice, which we could make out. When we checked the recorder, it captured a class A EVP saying, "I have heard of you often."

Time 11:17 p.m.

I was grabbed by something. On my left forearm, I could feel the hand wrap around my forearm and squeeze. It felt ice cold!

Time 11:40 p.m.

We move to center room to do a ghost box session directly over pit area. We could feel energy coming from under the floor. As I stood there, something grabbed at me, scratching my chest, where my protection metals were hanging — like it was actual trying to rip them off of me. Photos were taken, but they never showed up on either of the two investigators cameras.

Considering I looked at one of the pictures, on the view finder of one of the cameras, which I find odd to say the least!

Time 11:58 p.m.

Right after hearing a loud disembodied voice yell out, "Help," something grabbed/poked my left butt cheek forcibly!

Other Comments:

The things that happened to me before hand, on the day we were leaving to go to the house, and what has gone on with my leg since I have left this home, only makes me think in the back of my mind, is it is because I was at this home. Does it have something to do with it? I felt a strong, native presence on the property, and an almost evil feeling in the home. I say this, even though, when we toured the home, none of the investigators felt anything negative at all. However, the second time, we entered the home all that changed for us. This home is a great research facility. In our opinion, only seasoned investigators and teams should take on this task. Newbies beware! Respect it or suffer. It is a must, to make a tobacco offering, to the willow tree!! After only one night spent there, all investigators feel that it is a must, to return and spend at least 2 to 3 days here, doing research and investigating. This place is a must return for all involved!

CHAPTER 12

MELVIN BRAZZEL

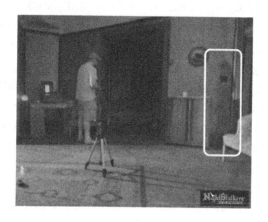

I first met Melvin Brazzel during an investigation at Octagon Hall in Kentucky. I had never met the man before he investigated my house. After talking at length with Melvin, I believe he is an honest and sincere person. He is a veteran and has skeptical attitude when it comes to investigating the paranormal. Make no bones about it, he is a straight shooter with nothing to gain personally from his investigations. He is an experienced person with numerous years and locations under his belt. The following is his experience and take on Willows Weep.

Phenomena as witnessed by Melvin Brazzell

My name is Melvin Brazzell. I have been investigating for around eight years now. Among the places I have been are Octagon Hall, Thomas House, Wheatland Plantation, Sloss Furnace, Benton Farms and various private residences. I am a proud member of Nightstalkers Paranormal Research Team. I am also a husband, father and grandfather, and a proud Vietnam veteran.

Cayuga, Indiana is the home of one of the most haunted locations I have ever investigated. Willows Weep has had its share of death and misery. After first arriving in late afternoon, did a preliminary walkthrough. At that time, no threatening or feelings of dread came upon me. By the time all equipment was set up, the house took an entirely different feeling, especially like someone had his or her eyes on you.

Several things happened that night that really stick out in my mind. During an EVP session in middle of the floor, directly above the pit area, a young girl's voice said, "HELP. " It was a Class A EVP. At the location over the pit, you can feel energy coming up from the floor.

Shadow figures were abounding in the house, constantly moving in and around various rooms, especially toward front of house. Footsteps, mist, knocks and orbs were numerous and happened all night. I don't put much emphasis on orbs, mainly because dust, moisture, bugs and other air-borne particles are most times confused for orbs. What I consider an orb is self-illuminated and moving in rapid movements.

During an outside investigation, voices were heard by Bear and myself. We knew we were not alone by any means. In one picture, I could make out red orbs, mist. These orbs were coming from the ground. Several pictures were made, and only one had all these anomalies in the same pictures. When I make pictures, I take three or four, without moving my camera. This way, I have something to compare with.

The ominous willow tree in front yard is quite creepy and should not be messed with. Is the Weep haunted? I must say YES!

CHAPTER 13

STEVE MILLER

The following is sent in from Steve Miller, who is a member of Night Stalkers Paranormal. I have only met Steve once, and it was after the he investigated Willows Weep with Barry Gaunt and Melvin. When documenting the goings on at the house, I wanted to hear many different people's take on the house -- the evidence they collected, if any, as well as their personal experiences. Some of the folks in this book I know very well. Some are acquaintances, and some I have never met personally. This aspect was very important to me, in order to have a fair cross section of different folks, who have investigated the house. The following is Steve's experience at the Weep.

Phenomena as witnessed by Steve Miller

When we arrived at Willows Weep, we pulled to the back of the building. While the team chatted with the caretaker, Rocky, I paid attention to the interesting architecture, with windows on every corner of its white exterior. Rocky took us inside to see the interior of the Weep. Initially, the house was quiet. However, when we got the equipment set up, the temperament of house changed. The others left to get supplies, while I set up the cameras for the investigation. I felt like something was curious about my presence. It stayed close; I could feel it spying on me. The Weep's inhabitants were aware of our intentions for the night. The night's investigation was riddled with sounds of knocks and footstep moving throughout the house. Our recorders picked up the sounds of the hidden voices beside us.

"You gonna hurt yourself," a man said, as we walked into the living room, to start our investigation. Later, a little girl responds,"It hurts," as we discuss a toy water gun, left behind on a table.

The entities of Willows Weep are not shy. The atmosphere was intense in the house that night. Only after packing everything up and leaving the property did that feeling finally disperse.

CHAPTER 14
NICOLE NOVELLE

Phenomena as witnessed by Nicole Novelle: Willows Weep- Trip One

When I first heard about Willows Weep, I instantly became enamored by it. I had to go -- it wasn't an option for me. At this time, Dave and I hosted a paranormal radio show together. We were always discussing paranormal anything and everything on air, as well as when we were off air. It was only natural, to call Dave, immediately after watching a video about the house. I told him he HAD to go watch it and he had to watch it RIGHT NOW! After completing the video, Dave called me back and I said, "Okay Dave, we have to go there!" Little did I realize, but my obsession with Willows Weep, had just begun. I begged Dave to figure out how to get us access to the house. Within hours, Dave called me back and said "Okay, you were serious right, Niki?" Of course I quickly replied "YESSS!" That's when Dave let me know that he talked to the owner at that time, Ms. Brenda, and she had granted us permission to come investigate Willows Weep.

When we arrived at the house, I was in awe, finally being at the place that I had only seen on the internet; that place that I couldn't stop thinking about, or talking about. I was really there. The strange architecture, of the house, seemed even stranger in person. Upon walking into the house, it was easy to say, within a matter of seconds, this place had an energy like nowhere I had ever been to before. It was dark inside. The air was musty and thick. You could tell that it had been some time since anyone had dared to enter. Looking around, you could almost feel the sadness that must have seeped into the walls. And you could feel, that the walls of this house, have absorbed all the despair from all that called this place home.

During Dave's and my investigation, we had many unexplained groans, thumps, knocks, growls and even distant disembodied voices. I felt as though someone/something had, at one point in the investigation, stabbed me in the back. We had an interesting flashlight session during which we were able to get confirmation of every single answer we received. We ran a spirit box, which we had an interaction with an intelligent entity, as well as something that was rather dark; even going as far as stating that we were directly communicating with Baphomet. Dave felt something come up from the floor, something that came with force. He even felt something touch his hand and immediately felt a sudden, distinct, cold breeze. There were so many other things that happened that night, that we were, and are still, unable to explain. I just knew, as I was packing up my equipment to leave, that this place seems to have "taken" a piece of me and I too have taken a piece of it. I knew this because it seriously had taken over my thoughts and became front and center for most all of my conversations. I knew I would be back again to explore and investigate this place. Again...it wasn't an option.

Shortly after returning home, Dave called me to let me know the owner at the time, Ms. Brenda, had called him. She told Dave that, a day after we had investigated the house, a couple had contacted her saying they were going to be in the neighborhood and wanted to know if they could stop by the house to walk through it. Ms. Brenda had given the couple her permission. The couple ran an audio recorder while they walked through, and they told Ms. Brenda, that they had picked up someone saying "Niki" repeatedly during their walk through the house. It seems as though maybe the house wanted me to come back as much as I wanted to.

Nicole Novelle's Return

I finally made it back to Willows Weep, this time accompanied by my dear friend and fellow investigator Jenna. The house had the same heavy feeling as we entered, and almost immediately the experiences began. I felt as though I was walking through spiderwebs that weren't there and I kept having something touch me. We had doors move on their own. EVPs, and batteries that were fully charged became drained before even being put into devices. Shortly before the end of our investigation, I had a particularly interesting encounter. Our cameras were placed in the room, where the blood-soaked chair is, and we were in the main living room. While conducting a session, I looked up, only to see what I thought was a living, breathing man, standing in front of the camera screen. I turned around, so to be able to see from where we were sitting. I jumped up, picking up a broken tripod, ready to "throw down" on this "intruder," only to find out that this was no living, breathing person; this was an entity, that was solid enough, to block my view of the camera's screen. I seriously was about to go after a person, that low and behold, was an entity. This experience was absolutely incredible.

I feel that there is something dark at Willows Weep, although I haven't quite put my finger on exactly what it may be. I would like to learn more as to what is occurring at the location. I feel that people may be subject to obtaining an attachment or possibly physical attacks, by unseen forces while at Willows Weep.

I feel as though I must return once again to Willows Weep. It's still on my mind often, and my obsession with this location has not at all lessened. I do not feel I will ever get over the hold this location has had on me, and I cannot wait to return and see what else the Weep has in store for me.

CHAPTER 15
"JENNA"

I've known Jenna for a few years now. I met her through my friend Nicole Novelle. Through talking to them both, I discovered that she has done quite a bit of research and behind-the-scenes things of haunted locations. She has a passion for the field and is a very honest type of person. She is limited in her field experience, as she has just begun her journey into that aspect of investigating. However, she has been working with Nicole, a very experienced person, as well as a few others out there. She is very good at audio and video review, and is learning the proper techniques of investigation. This is her experience and account from her investigation with Nicole at the Weep.

Phenomena as witnessed by Jenna

The first time I heard about Willows Weep, it was from my good friend and fellow investigator Nicole Novelle. She had gone on a trip to the Midwest with Dave, and ever since that trip, she had a downright obsession about the location. She came back from the trip and told me of the dark history, and what she and Dave had experienced. Immediately I was intrigued. The more she told me, the more I hoped, that someday, I would get to go there myself.

That day came in June of 2017. Nicole and I were planning a paranormal adventure, that would take us across to the Midwest and back again, spanning 18 days. I begged her to have the Weep as one of our many locations. After speaking to Ms. Brenda, it was arranged, and we set off to one of the darkest locations, I have ever been to. Prior to our arrival, Ms. Brenda explained she wouldn't be able to meet us, and we were just to go to the house ourselves. This was fine, but I was sad, as I was looking forward to meeting her. As we pulled up, I could see why this house would intimidate someone. The exterior, even in daylight, is very ominous and foreboding. At the time, being a novice investigator with only a couple of investigations, on location, under my belt, I wasn't nervous per se, but on guard.

Nicole told me "You might want to run a recorder as you enter and also video-record your feelings as you do your initial walkthrough." I agreed and she went in the house first. I remember it as if I was going into the house right now. As soon as you go over the threshold into the first little area, that leads to the kitchen, you notice it; the darkness. And it surrounds you. The way the house was built, it didn't really allow for that much natural light inside, and that added to the creep factor. Nicole started to give me a tour of the place, telling me what happened here and there, when she and Dave had visited. I remember her asking (the house or the entities within) "Do you remember me?" It was after that question that she got her response and she was touched for the first time. Two minutes in and there was already touching. I knew at this point this house was no joke.

The house had been locked up, for some time before we came and, as a result, the air inside was heavy and gave you a feeling, as if you were walking through pea soup. It made it harder to breath. She had asked me how the house felt. I remember saying just that, "It's thick in here; the air is really thick." She agreed and we went through the room that holds the infamous chair -- the one with the bloodstains from a suicide many years earlier, otherwise known as the death chair. As we walked into the next big open-area room, I decided to veer off into the room to the left. This room had two massive wooden doors being held open by boulders. As I stepped inside, Nicole said she just got touched again and then, immediately after, the door on my right moved forward. This was the same door being held open by a massive rock. Nicole said, "Did you see that?" I said, "No, but I heard it." I was focused on looking around in the room, at the couch etc. and she was looking in towards me. I remember thinking at the time, that this was going to be an investigation I won't soon forget.

As it got later and we set up, we noticed, despite fresh batteries in all of our equipment, we could not keep anything charged. Batteries were dying left and right on everything. We were supposed to livestream that night and couldn't even get a signal out to do so. We called Dave and he agreed, that stuff, is typical of that location. Despite not being able to livestream, we continued to film and used the ghost box and do EVP sessions. Our EVPs, that we were getting from there, were amazing, and I really do think, we were speaking with the man who shot himself in the house.

As the night wore on and battery after battery was dying immediately after being put in the camera, I knew something was going to happen. Something was getting charged up to make an appearance and sure enough it soon did. After one EVP session, I looked over at Nicole and I saw her tense up as she looked toward the room that contains that chair. In that room, she had a camera placed that was facing the chair, and that was one of the cameras that was continuously losing battery. The next thing I saw, was Nicole grabbing a tripod like a weapon. I asked her, "What's going on? What do you see?" and she said tensely, "Don't you see it over there, by the camera?" I looked over and I saw exactly what she was talking about. There in front of the camera, was a black mass, completely blocking out the screen of the camera, that she had facing us. She continued to describe what she saw. She told me she saw a figure of a man, with a T-shirt on, standing over by the camera. It was so realistic to her, that she thought someone had come in, while we were doing our session, and tried to break in. I didn't see his shirt outline, but I saw the mass covering the camera screen and then, when it was gone, I saw the screen again. Shortly after that incident, it was getting towards early morning and we started wrapping up.

If you ever get a chance to go to this house, it will have an effect on you. It is dark. It is no joke. It will pull you back time and time again. It will call to you in your sleep, like it calls to me. I want to return, and I will. When I do it will be ready.

CHAPTER 16
Daywalkers Paranormal
John and Debbie Holiday

I first met John and Debbie, during a meet and greet, the day I became the owner of the house. I knew who they were, as they have been around the paranormal circles, for quite some time. They have a great reputation, as being skeptical-minded, and will pull no punches, if they think a location is not what it is said to be. It was only a short time after I had met them, when they approached me about investigating the house. I agreed to let them investigate it, as I was curious to see what they would experience, and capture there. I value their opinions and thoughts about the house. I also wholeheartedly believe, what they experienced at the house, was real, beyond a shadow of a doubt. The following is they experienced as they occurred, as told by them.

Phenomena as witnessed by John and Debbie Holiday

Debbie and I arrived at the small, run-down location with its oddly shaped, structured house. The property has a creepy vibration to it. As we stood out front and admired the house, we noticed the large willow tree with its branches blowing in a slight breeze. Debbie asked me not to touch the willow tree due to the legend associated with the tree. The legend states, "Those that touch the willow tree, will suffer some form of misfortune." So of course, I walked up to the tree, stood beneath its branches and wondered what ghostly entities were watching me there. After a few deep breaths and a silent prayer, I reached out my hand and saying quietly, 'I mean no harm,' I touched the tree. I heard Debbie shout to me, "I can't believe you touched that haunted willow." I was quite happy to walk away from the willow tree.

We walked the property, absorbing the energy that flowed from the house and the grounds. We felt someone, or something, was watching us. Debbie's son Devin took IR photos. Debbie walked around taking digital photos while I captured video.

We were waiting to gain entry, because we arrived early. We decided to fly our drone over the property. In a few minutes, the previous owner, who just happened to be driving by, saw us walking around the property and approached us, asking if we had permission to be there. We explained that Dave Spinks gave us permission to be there. The previous owner then recounted her experiences inside the house to us. She was glad that Dave now owned the property. The toll the house, along with its dark entities, had taken on her and her family had been too much.

Eventually, we entered the house and at first it seemed unremarkable. The house was dark, gloomy, and dusty from being closed all winter. We were the first ones to enter for months. The air inside was musty and smelled.

We were there to investigate and to do a "Day-walkers Paranormal" live radio show with Dave Spinks as our guest on "Paranormal King" network.

Our show was to start at 8 p.m. eastern time, so we were eager to get things rolling.

As we stood in the kitchen area, the vibration of the house seemed lighter, less threatening. But as we walked deeper into the house, we could feel the environment shift. The house became darker, heavier, and less welcoming, and each of us could feel that we were being observed from the deeper part of the house. Someone or something was observing us. Being observed made each of us feel tense but, as investigators, also excited to see what might develop.

Right from the start, we had trouble establishing a Wi-Fi connection. We contacted Dave via our cell phones to ask for assistance. We checked and double-checked everything, but something did not want us going live that night, with Dave, to talk about Willows Weep.

There was nothing technically wrong with the Wi-Fi, other than a supernatural force, that prevented us from communicating with Dave. Our radio show was cancelled due to technical problems. This entity would disrupt our equipment from this moment on. It seemed to enjoy toying with us, to watch our reaction.

Things were heating up as the house became alive, so we informed Debbie's young son Devin to stay near us. The kitchen area seemed to be an island of refuge, whereas the rest of the house was an invitation to trouble. Debbie retrieved the X-Cam SLS camera to do a sweep of the house. The SLS stands for Structured Light Sensor. SLS is a scanning camera, that will capture and understand the environment. The X-Cam SLS is based around an advanced SLS as well as additional sensor inputs. All of the data is gathered and displayed in real time. We wanted to see if the SLS would capture any anomalies. As soon as Debbie would turn the SLS camera on, and enter the living room, something would turn the camera off. This pattern repeated over and over, until we asked permission to film throughout the house. Finally, slowly, Debbie inched her way through the house. Anomalies were detected in the bathroom and rear living room.

We also heard disembodied voices. One was female that came from the bathroom. She seemed to be lingering in the bathtub. We tried to get her to join us outside of the bathroom, but to no avail. All night long, she would trigger the REM Pod that we placed in the bathroom, but only if we walked away.

The other, darker disembodied voice was male, and he was the entity that seemed to rule the house. This entity moved freely throughout the house, had zero fear of us and seemed to relish toying with us. I question, even now, if the male is even human, but instead, something much older and darker.

After the SLS sweep was complete, we tried to make contact by using the ghost box in the living room, but this male entity did not want to verbally communicate this way. Instead, he moved along the walls in shadow form. He made knocking and scratching noises near us.I believe he was enjoying trying to scare us. It was creepy.

At one point, I sent Debbie and Devin outside for a break, while I took additional photos inside the house. I wanted to see if this thing would show itself. As I started to take photos, I thought I felt the presence of a little girl. It wasn't a little girl. This thing had morphed itself and deceived me by changing its energy. After I realized the deception, and as I filmed near the very back small room, this entity ran up on me from behind and my whole body shook. It was a terrifying moment. All I could do was say, "Holy, Holy, Holy." I immediately backed out of the room. I could feel goose bumps on my arms, and the hairs on my arms standing straight up. I have investigated for twenty years, and maybe twice, have I ever been so fooled and frightened.

I needed a break to gather myself. I understood we were dealing with something evil and we had to be very careful. I explained to Debbie my encounter and I remember Debbie being shocked by how rattled I was.We understood the game now, so we knew the rules were different now. We decided not to be intimidated because we knew darker entities feed and gain strength from fear.

In the living room at Willows Weep sits the suicide chair. This chair is old and covered in blood. The chair sits in the corner of the room. I sat in the chair with my cell phone and played a pre-recorded sound of a shotgun blast. We hoped for an audible response, since we had heard that a resident of the house had shot himself and died in this chair. Debbie and I noticed that I was wearing the same hat that sat above the chair and we thought that was odd. I had just gotten the hat a few days before. After I played the gun blast recording, the REM Pod in the bathroom alarmed and the audio recording picked up the sounds of a shotgun cocking.

We decided to do another SLS sweep of the house. Debbie would sweep as I followed behind her and filmed. As she entered the living room, the SLS captured an anomaly standing toward her left as we passed by. At this moment, something turned my camera off. I made a comment about my camera being turned off, and our recorder picked up a male voice saying happily, "Yea, I did it." I said to it, "You don't like being filmed?" Audible response, "Yeah."

The oppressive feelings we felt, as the evening and night wore on, began to bother us. We were uniquely aware, that our encounters with this entity, were something extraordinary and dangerous. We understood why people would harm themselves here. The darkness, sadness, anger, rage, and hopelessness attach themselves to anyone inside the house. Although this thing would talk to us, we understood that, over time, he would grind down even the strongest mind, the strongest spiritually grounded individual, and destroy them. We felt we needed a salt bath and a spiritual cleansing. The risk for us, was becoming so intrigued by the entity, that we would open ourselves to being harmed.We decided not to stay too much longer.

We agreed to attempt an Ovilus-5 session in the death chair. This time, Debbie would sit in the chair. We would both ask questions while I filmed the session. The Ovilus-5 converts environmental readings into words. Debbie and I have had great results using this device. Debbie turned the device on. The Ovilus-5 said, "Relax." Debbie asked for the entity's name? "Ron." "Heyyyyyy." The bathroom REM Pod alarm sounded again. Debbie asked additional questions, receiving no responses. Then Ovilus said, "Less friendly."

We decided to change things up and pay respects to those who died inside the residence. Debbie continued to use the Ovilus-5 while I played the "Lord's Prayer" through my cell phone. Then the temperature dropped, and the house was much colder. Right before we started, the Ovilus-5 said, "Satan." I play the Lord's Prayer audio recording. The Ovilus-5 said "Confess."

After this, we started to pack our equipment and prepare to leave. However, this thing wasn't finished with us yet. As Debbie stepped out of the house and turned the corner, a black shadow figure approached her and tried to block her view of our vehicle.

We were glad to leave. Once back at home, we saged ourselves and our vehicle.

Willows Weep is not for the faint of heart.

CHAPTER 17
THE ORIGINAL PARASISTERS®

The first time I met Tina and Jackie was at an event in Illinois. They had a table near mine and we struck up some conversation. I again saw them at another event in Indiana, and we became better acquaintances. It was at this time, that they invited me to be a part of an event they were putting on in Fort Wayne, Indiana. We had talked about Willows Weep around that time and discussed investigating it together. They had informed me of their experiences there, and I told them of mine at the time. On Halloween 2016, we met up at the house and investigated it together. Little did I know at this time, that I would become the owner.

Tina and Jackie are very well-known investigators and one of the best teams I've worked with. Some of their cases have been featured on TV, and they have been around for many years. I value their opinion plus trust their data and evidence collection, as if it were my own. Below are their thoughts and experiences on Willows Weep.

Phenomena as witnessed by The Original ParaSisters®

Upon our arrival at "Willows Weep," Cayuga, Indiana, the feeling in the air was heavy. At this point, we realized that we were in for an eventful evening.

As we arrived in this town, we saw an old wooden directional sign pointing in all directions as well as an old covered bridge. Also located in this town is "The Eugene Cemetery," which sits about one block from our destination. This little town exudes character and charm, and nestled in a quiet area amongst other homes sits our destination, Willows Weep.

We were immediately met by the owner, Brenda Zimmerman Johnson, along with her team: Danville Paranormal out of Danville, Illinois; and "S.P.A.D.D" out of Indianapolis. Brenda shared a little history of the home, and the two teams, shared some experiences they have had there.

Brenda explained that there had been a few deaths and suicides in this home, and that a former tenant even attempted suicide, which she feels may have some association with the feeling of the home. The teams went on to tell us about their experiences while investigating Willows Weep. They said they heard growls, doors slamming shut on their own, floors shake, footsteps, bangs, knocks, unusual noises, and noticed smells. They seemed to think that, whatever was dwelling there, did not seem very friendly at all. Both teams have had experiences every time they have held an investigation there.

During our initial walkthrough of the home, one of our more sensitive team members picked up on some emotions, that she described as being from "an older woman in a house dress." It was then confirmed, by Brenda, that there had been an older woman who had died there in the home. She also picked up on a man struggling to get out of a chair. Again, Brenda confirmed that there was a man, who did commit suicide, in the home. We knew, at this time, we were going to have a very interesting night of investigating. After everyone had gone and we were the only ones remaining, we set up. It was time to investigate.

Willows Weep, built in 1890, does have a very heavy feeling about it. The entire setup of the home is very unusual. The floors at Willows Weep shake very easily when anyone walks on them, and when there are passing trains. The vibrations can be felt upon first hearing the train, even though it is a few miles away. The floors also will give a vertigo effect.

Our adventures there began almost immediately. We heard growls, which we captured on our EVPs. We saw black masses; we heard knocks and bangs. We heard, what one would describe, as someone snoring; we could hear breathing. We had pants being tugged on, people's arms being touched, and, what one would describe as a "tickle" feeling. One of our investigators had a bracelet on, and it seemed as though someone was playing with it on her wrist. We had brushing against our legs. We could hear a dragging sound.

At one point in the evening, we decided to put down some baby powder on the floor. Someone felt their leg get brushed and a cold wind breeze went by, and when we turned our flashlights on, there were two bare footprints in the baby powder! A right foot, left foot, and then it stops. The curvature of the foot and the outline of the toes could also be recognized. We did get pictures of these footprints. The footprints will be on our websites for everyone to see.

In conclusion: This home most definitely has paranormal activity going on! Our most compelling evidence is the footprints, which we could not debunk. We know that no team member was walking around barefoot, and we also know that the footprints just stop. That, along with the fact that we had just felt someone walk by, makes it pretty strong evidence. The footprints were small, but not of a child; maybe those of a small woman. The EVPs we caught of the "growl," which we all heard, was confirmed.

A few days after the investigation, we received a phone call from Brenda saying she saw footprints in the baby powder in the bedroom, and they stopped at the wall. We assured her that none of us were barefoot, and that we also had caught footprints in the baby powder, but ours were in the living room.

Although we were not able to find the source of the growling, we heard, we did not feel threatened by it either. We did get hits on our K-2 meters, a few times, when we would speak of the man that had committed suicide there. We had temperature drops of 5 degrees when asked.

Unfortunately, our video evidence was of no use, because of our use of baby powder, which caused too many orbs, making the video hard to see. With the constant brushing against the legs all night, one might also wonder if there is a spirit of a cat there in the home.

We had an experience of the feeling of our legs being brushed against at different points in the evening.

We do believe there is paranormal activity going on at Willows Weep. It was a thrill that did not disappoint us, and is the kind of investigation that we wish we could experience everywhere we go.

CHAPTER 18
PARANORMAL INDY
JEFF PHILLIPS

I first met Jeff Phillips at an event I was attending in Indiana, a few years prior to becoming the owner of Willows Weep. Upon having a conversation with him, he told me of a location he and his team manage called "The Guyer Opera House." He was quick to invite me to investigate the location. After hearing him speak of the history and some of the paranormal evidence he gathered at the location, I accepted. Jeff and his team are very good investigators. I have seen some of their captures and evidence; It is some of the best I have seen. I wanted him to experience the Weep for himself and get his take on the place, not only his paranormal opinion but also, with Jeff having been in the insurance industry for over 40 years. I wanted his professional opinion on the construction of the house. Below are Jeff's thoughts and experiences of Willows Weep.

Phenomena as witnessed by Jeff Phillips

My name is Jeff Phillips. I am with an investigating group out of Indianapolis, Indiana called Paranormal Indy. We have been involved with the paranormal for approximately 10 years. Paranormal Indy has conducted investigations in: New Jersey, Pennsylvania, Ohio, Florida, North Carolina, Colorado, and Indiana. We are affiliated with the "Guyer Opera House" in Lewisville, Indiana. It is a functioning theater where plays are currently shown. "The Guyer Opera House" was built in 1901, and has a long history of paranormal activity.

Over the course of the years, we have heard of Willows Weep from others in the paranormal community. It has been on our bucket list to investigate. On October 27, 2017, I had the opportunity to investigate with Dave Spinks. I will say it was quite an experience. I believe it is great to investigate with other paranormal enthusiasts, to observe and share different investigative techniques and equipment used. I believe Dave is one of the best investigators I have seen. Dave shared some of the history of Willows Weep, which is very intriguing to say the least.

Upon entering the house, there was an immediate feeling of heaviness and, not to be overly dramatic, but I would say dread. I was quite nervous and apprehensive.

But first, I would like to comment on Willows Weep and then I will share some of my experiences and observations.

This is a very interesting structure. As is known, the original structure is built in the shape of a cross. That in itself is somewhat peculiar. On one hand, the design would make sense, having the common living area in the center and the living quarters branching off of the common area. On the other hand, one questions if there is a different reason for the design.

One of the most interesting parts of the construction is in the common area. At ceiling height, in the four corners there are what I would refer to as "build outs." These are triangular-shaped and are symmetrical. My first thought was they are bulkheads for the HVAC metal ductwork. However, upon further evaluation that was ruled out, as there does not appear to be ductwork in the attic. They appear to be constructed of lathe and plaster, as are the sidewalls and the ceiling. That is an appropriate construction technique for the time in which the home was built. The question remains as to why the "build outs" are there. It could be that they were added as a decorative touch to the common area. They appear to have no real function.

My first thought was perhaps they coincided with the navigational direction of north, south, east and west. But after checking a compass, that theory did not prove to be factual.

During the course of the investigation, I stood in the center of the common area room. I was equal distance from the four "build outs." I immediately began to feel differently. The sensations are hard to describe, but I would say it was feelings of being light-headed, dizzy, tingly, and a feeling of swaying or movement. I know I was standing still, but I was having difficulty remaining standing and still. It was quite interesting.

My "day job" of 40 years is that of an insurance adjuster. With this, I have been in hundreds if not thousands of homes and buildings over the years. I have never seen construction like that at Willows Weep. I have never experienced feelings like those of Willows Weep just due to standing in the center of a room. I am not saying that the construction contributes to any paranormal activity, that may be present in the structure, or that it influenced my physical reactions. But I am not saying that it did not. Is the design and build simply creative on behalf of the original owners and builders? Is there something sinister behind this design? The answers have yet to be determined.

I would recommend to any paranormal group to investigate Willows Weep.
Perhaps the answers to the questions are with the next investigation.

CHAPTER 19
NO NONSENSE PARANORMAL
BRIAN AND MARLENA CORNS

I first met Brian and Marlena Corns of "No Nonsense Paranormal" the day I became the new owner of Willows Weep. I found them to be credible people and enjoyed our conversations that day. They had explained that they had several intense experiences in the house during their investigations at Willows Weep. Below are their experiences as explained by them.

Phenomena as witnessed by "No Nonsense Paranormal"

During our first visit to Willows Weep, it turned out to be one of the most active places we have ever been. Although we heard many of the stories of the occurrences at Willows Weep, we always maintain skepticism during our investigations. Almost immediately during our first visit to the house, we heard a pill bottle rattle, and movement along with more unexplained movement in the front two rooms. After settling in, we decide to do some experiments with different paranormal tools, having some good results with all of them.

While taking a break in the barn, we heard a loud sound inside the house. We got up, to go into the house to investigate the sound. Once near the rear entrance to the house, my wife saw what she described as a "creeper-style" entity that was "sucked into the house." This same entity was seen again, later in the investigation, by a different investigator, on the other side (driveway side) of the house.

That night ended in a Ganzfeld experiment, conducted by myself, while sitting in the chair in the house. It is a known fact that an individual had commented suicide in the house. While conducting the experiment, I began to have the sensation of thick liquid running down the right side of my neck. This is the same side, where the majority of the blood stains are located, on the chair that the man died in. After being in the Ganzfeld experiment for about 20 minutes, I felt like there was a dark figure about seven feet tall (I'm 6' 5") coming in from the living room area. This was backed up, by two others in the room, who saw this same dark figure coming into the room. This resulted in the end of the experiment and the investigation.

Another occasion at Willows Weep was very intense. It was about two two years after our first investigation, during a para-con on the property. We had put together a group investigation on this occasion. While inside, six people heard the pill bottle rattling, along with unexplained movement, voices, and moans.

While sitting in the side room — which would be the left part of the cross-shaped house — I felt a depression on the couch beside me, as if someone had sat down next to me, but no one was there. A few seconds later, it stood up. Several people in the room ,looking in, said that the window, behind the couch I was sitting on, blacked out, as if someone stood up, causing the light coming in from outside to be blocked out. It was all confirmed by several people in the house.

The large doors inside the house, leading into the rooms, are held open by chucks of concrete. While in the same room as the shadow figure, but after it seemed to disappear, one of the other investigators walked into the room with me and the door slammed shut on him hitting his arm. We spent the next 20 minutes, having three different people, walk by the door in the same fashion as he did, in attempt to find a reasonable cause and explanation for the door slamming on his arm. I weigh 275 pounds. He weighs 120 pounds. Nothing we tried caused the door to shut, let alone slam shut.

CHAPTER 20
EXPLORERS OF SPIRIT PHENOMENA

Terri Rohde, Tracy Watts, Ken Head "Doc", and I have been friends since we met at an event held at the former "Seven Sisters Inn" back in 2014. We became friends very quickly, and soon we were conducting joint investigations together. They are very meticulous when conducting evidence review, and serious Investigators. I have observed them firsthand while investigating with them. I am glad to call them my friends. I knew they had investigated Willows Weep, before I became the owner, and I asked them if they would like to contribute, what they had experienced at the house," for the book. Tragically in 2017, my friend and Terri's husband, Doc, passed away suddenly. I was proud to call him a friend. Doc was the kind of guy who would help someone with no questions asked; a truly golden-hearted person. Doc, you are missed tremendously, and I am sure we will meet again someday. Below is testimony as told by Terri and Tracy of their experiences at Willows Weep.

Phenomena as witnessed by "Explorers of Spirit Phenomena"

We were on a paranormal road trip in the summer of 2016. We had just finished two nights of investigating at "Sedamsville Rectory," and we were heading to Peoria to investigate Pollack Hospital. We wanted to stop at a halfway point, and were hoping to find another haunted location. We logged onto the "Haunted Journeys" app and searched for haunted spots in Indiana. This place called Willows Weep popped up. Having no idea if the place was still allowing investigations, or if it was even open, we found a contact number and phoned. When the owner answered, she told us the home wasn't booked and we could come and investigate.

When we arrived, the first thing we noticed was the large weeping willow tree outside. The owner of the house walked over to meet us. She lived next door. She gave us a quick overview of where we could go to use the restroom, as the house had no running water or electricity. She told us little to nothing about the home's history, except that a couple of folks had passed in the house and they believed one was a suicide.

We grabbed our gear, anxious to begin. When we entered the house, we noticed that the home was in the shape of a pentagon, with a room at each of the flat sides. All the windows and doors were in corners of the house. We had never seen anything like this before. We immediately had goose bumps as we walked through the home, and the atmosphere was very dark, far creepier than any we had encountered to this point on our trip. This is saying a lot, as we had already investigated Bobby Mackey's, "Benton Farms," and "Sedamsville Rectory" in the past week. We lit candles around the home, to give us light, and began the night with a dowsing rod session in the living room. We received a "yes" answer, from the rods, when we asked if there were spirits in the home, and if there had been a suicide there. But the rods stated, it was a woman, not a man who took their life. During the session, we also saw energy swirling up from around the rods.

We decided this place was a perfect spot for a collective consciousness activity. We phoned our fellow paranormal investigator, psychic, author, and remote viewer, George Lopez. We started the Facebook

Live session by asking the spirits to manipulate the candle flames, since the air was extremely still and stagnant. The house was also rather hot. At 10:44 p.m., a light anomaly was seen on the screen. A remote psychic, who was viewing, picked up on a female spirit, with a facial deformity of some type. Terri felt a spirit enter the room. George wrote down what was he was picking up, remotely, from the spirit. They both described the spirit as an Amish man, about 5' 8," with dark hair. We felt he could be a pastor. We got more goose bumps and Terri got the name Frank. Another psychic, viewing remotely, got the name Abe. During a follow-up EVP session, we captured a whisper on the voice recorder, when we asked about the name Abe or Abraham.

During the second collective consciousness experiment, we asked the spirits to manifest a breeze and move the flame on the candle which was located on the table. As we all focused on that, the candle flame moved toward Terri, as if bending. Light anomalies were seen by the viewers during this session. George then asked the viewers, to put themselves there, at Willows Weep, and manifest a sound. We then heard a tap, and the flame, from the candle on the floor, grew three times taller.

We felt compelled to move into the room, with paneling, that had a burn spot on the wall. We both agreed that there was a negative energy in that room. We decided to do an EVP session there, by the burn spot on the wall. The closet door, in that room, was a third of the way closed when we came into the room. During the session it completely closed, but we did not hear a thing. Cheryl, one of the remote viewers, felt bad energy at the closet. Terri felt the energy of a fight. One of the remote psychics felt the energy was from a father/son fight during which the door had been broken when there was yelling and pounding on upon it. George felt there was a portal there. The burn spot on the wall seemed to resemble a ram's head, and one of the viewers, stated that they sensed an inhuman presence in the home, before even seeing that spot. During a second EVP session at 11:24 p.m., Tracy heard footsteps. Terri heard them on the recorder during playback. Terri was covered in goose bumps. After the session, we continued to hear faint, far-away footsteps.

Next, we moved into the blue room. We called it that because there was blue paneling on the walls. Terri placed her hand on the wall and said she felt a child's presence; a small, dark-haired boy. George asked Terri what she felt or what she could see, in her mind's eye (psychometry), in that room. Terri said she felt sickness, sadness, white sheets, and an old-fashioned water pitcher by the bed. George asked, "Where on the wall is the mirror? Put your hand where the mirror is." He wrote down that the mirror was over Terri's left shoulder. Terri placed her hand on the wall, in the exact same spot that George had predicted.

As we moved through the rest of the house, we noticed the room with the Christmas tree in it. It felt different from the other rooms; much lighter and airier. It seemed to us, like that room, was not a part of the original house. Perhaps that room had been added later.

We found an old photo album, in a box, on the floor. Terri opened it, to a photo, that was the spitting image of Terri's mother when she was younger. As we were looking through the photo album, we felt like we were being watched. One of the remote viewers commented that they felt we were being followed. We flipped through the photo album and came to a photo of a man and a child. We felt that it was the man who was following us. George felt, that the woman of the house, was watching us. He felt she was very orderly and organized. She may have been upset that we were going through her things.

It was now after 1 a.m. We moved to the room with the blue rocking chair. A remote viewer had told us, early in the night, that there was strong energy associated with that chair. We got the feeling, that the blue chair, had belonged to the woman of the house. We decided to do an EVP session at the chair. As George was asking questions during the EVP session, the candle flame flickered and static came from the phone, even though the phone was on mute. Terri decided to sit in the chair, to see if she could sense anything. She felt that a woman had sat in that chair, while listening to the radio, and doing something with yarn like knitting or crocheting.

As the night turned to morning, the house continued to drain our equipment and phone batteries. We had to utilize several portable power supplies for the phones. Two power supplies, that were at 100% charge, went to nothing in just about 15 minutes.

While we were putting new batteries into our meters, we noticed a display case, full of items that had been left by investigators and visitors to the house. We were surprised to see a brick, from "Peoria Hospital," in the case, as that was our next stop on our paranormal road trip. We decided to conduct an EVP session near the case, and as we were talking, about the items in the case, the candle flame in the living room flickered back and forth like crazy. This seemed impossible, as there was no air moving in the house at all. So we did an experiment, to see how much air or motion it would take, to make the flame flicker that way. It took us flailing our arms, wildly over the candle, to make it move in any way, like it was moving. Some unknown force was acting on that candle. Another brand-new taper candle, burned all the way down to almost nothing, and there was no wax at all, remaining anywhere. That is not possible.

It is hard to describe, the energy in that house, when we entered that evening. It felt like we were in another dimension, a time warp. The house was so dark and still, it was like a tomb. There were even black sheets of plastic covering the windows, so even moonlight could not seep in. It was the creepiest we had ever felt, on an investigation. As the hours passed and we spent more time in the house, the energy in the living room finally shifted from dark and oppressive to calmer, lighter. In the years since, that night at Willows Weep, the only time we have experienced as dark a presence, was when we investigated the "Bellaire House" in Ohio.

CHAPTER 21
BARRY GAUNT'S SECOND INVESTIGATION

Deacon Casey Scruggs

My friend and fellow investigator, Barry Gaunt, had already made one trip to Willows Weep to conduct an investigation. Immediately after his first visit to my house, he contacted me saying that he and his team, had experienced some significant phenomena. He asked if they could go back, a second time, to conduct a longer and more in-depth investigation of the property. I was more than happy to oblige. Barry asked if he could bring along a trusted clergy member, on the second investigation, to get an impression of what that clergy member felt was going on in the house. I liked the idea. I told him absolutely, and that I welcomed the idea. The date was set for March of 2019. The following, is testimony from Deacon Casey Scruggs on his impressions of the Weep and his experiences while there. What transpired with him on the property is very telling.

Phenomena as witnessed by Deacon Casey Scruggs

I had been contacted by Barry Gaunt, who I work with performing clergy duties, such as house blessings, council, and evidence review. Barry inquired about me, accompanying his team, to a location known as Willows Weep. I was to walk through the house with them and give them my general feelings, as to what may be lurking within the home. I obliged and made the trip with him and team.

While at the house, I was talking with a friend, Kathleen Cowley. We have been friends for a few years, and as far as her gift of sight, it has been accurate. The following is what she texted to me as to what she was picking up on from the location:

"it has awful energy. "

"didn't like what I saw"

"I saw a man, standing with a pitchfork or something, just staring straight ahead, like he had (been) traumatized, blood everywhere, I have no idea what it means. There was a look of horror on his face, like he was in shock"

She went on to say that she didn't intentionally connect with the visions; that they were just coming to her. She continued by saying, that she felt as if there was some kind of "energy loop," that was causing bad things to occur at the house. She also was picking up on an overwhelming sense of doom, that is supernatural in nature, like some sort of a curse.

She believed she saw someone standing behind me. The person's name was Ann, and she was asking about her child. At this point, I didn't have any information about specific children that once resided in the location. However, I did find out Jesse's wife was named MaryAnn.

Upon my first walkthrough, I felt the change in energy and temps in the home. The team had gone back outside to finish setting up the equipment. I looked at the kitchen, and then went into the next room, inside the house, and stood completely still. There was a "boom," that emanated from underneath the floor, that shook the entire house. I heard the items in the display case shake as well. I went outside to check with Bear, Melvin, and Steve. They did not hear or feel the boom, but the audio recorder was set up at the time so they have the evidence.

Later, while outside looking around, I noticed a rod sticking out of the dirt. Pulling it out
and cleaning it off a bit, I immediately recognized it as a pitchfork. Immediately, I was reminded of what Kathleen had said, about seeing a man holding a pitchfork coming through to her. The style and age, on this particular pitchfork, indicated that it was not made in any recent years, and appeared to be very old. Part of me feels that it "wanted to be found."

Ms. Cowley also mentioned an "Esther," and a woman looking outside, as the chickens rustled, appearing to be in the same trance-like state, as she mentioned the guy in overalls, with the pitchfork, was. She stated she believed that "whatever" is in the house draws, in people, and that trance-like state takes over. She stated that the guy eaten by hogs possibly "let it happen." She also mentioned someone, with a butcher-block table, cutting a finger off in a trance-like state.

The investigation revealed: many light anomalies acting in an intelligent manner, equipment responded to questions on command, (flashlights, meters), many EVPs, and shadow figures. The entities, seemed to not particularly like me as clergy, so I removed myself from the house during a session, and the team stated, many more spirits vocalized, especially the ones of female persuasion. When I returned, there was an audible word "FUCK," as if a spirit or entity was displeased that I had returned inside the house.

While observing one of the cameras on night vision, I did see a spirit figure, sitting next to team member Melvin, on the leather couch (they have the evidence). And during one session, team member Barry stated that he got "cold on top of his head" and seemed to fall asleep. Later, back in the place, we set up equipment and he seemed, to me, distracted and withdrawn; different than his normal personality. I immediately laid a hand on his head and prayed. The feeling he was experiencing, went away instantaneously, and he was back to normal personality.

This was a very interesting and intense place, with a lot of activity. The feeling and the interactive spirits are real, in my humble opinion. During one session, Melvin stated a shadow, was in the Christmas tree room, approaching me, and the proximity meter went off immediately. The voices heard where anything from a distant, sounding female voice (multiple female voices) to a more aggressive male voice.

Deacon, Casey Scruggs OSB
615-598-7950
thebenedictine@outlook.com

CHAPTER 22
CONCLUSION

When conducting any investigations, one must always investigate possible reasons or events in the history of the location itself, or even the surrounding area, that may be a possible contributing factor in causing paranormal phenomena. In my search, I discovered several disturbing events, that may be significant to the house. Even though these factors are subjective and circumstantial in nature, as paranormal Investigators sometimes we must think outside the box.

An interesting aspect of many haunted locations, being investigated today, is that many have ties to being on sacred Native American land or very near sacred Native American land. Vermillion County is no exception. The

Mound Builders, are said to be the first known occupants on the land, where the house known as Willows Weep, sits. The largest mound, that is most often referenced, is one that is located southwest of Hazel Bluff, near Brouilletts Creek. It is 12.5 feet high, more than 300 feet long, and some 20 feet wide. Artifacts that have been unearthed are dated at more than 1,000 years old.

It is thought by some, that the ancient Mound Builders, were driven from the area by Native Americans. The ancient ones, were known to have created great cities, that encompassed vast expanses of land. Some of the modern Native Americans, were thought to have captured females from the ancient ones and wed them; thus some of the modern tribes carry on some of the ways of Mound Builders. The bodies of the dead, were often buried inside the mounds, and most of them were people of significance.

Most of the native tribes were nomadic, moving with the seasons and with game herds. The name they used, for the present day Wabash River, was Wahbahshikka. It was also called The Red Earth or Vermilion due to the rich, red color of the earth from the mineral deposits. They used the red earth for dying various items.

Over time, the French came in droves, which put a crimp on the hunting and caused many battles between the French and various native tribes. Eventually, treaties were signed. One such treaty, that was penned in 1809, was known as the "Treaty of Fort Wayne" and formed an invisible line, that runs through the central part of Vermillion County, to this day.

The legend of a chief, known as Little Turtle, who ruled over the Miami tribe, said that he did not trust the white man's surveying equipment, and only trusted a line, created by the shadow of a spear, that was thrown into the ground, at 10 o'clock in the morning. That line has caused many headaches for surveyors and mapmakers over the years.

As with many of the haunted locations that have Native American ties, it is thought to be a possibility, that the spirits are upset that sacred land has been desecrated by white settlers. The battles between the settlers and natives have also created a dark stain on the land. Many deaths occurred as a result of these battles, and the energy is most likely negative in nature. As an investigator, all this can be relevant, in the possible causes, of paranormal phenomena.

Some other noteworthy things, that may be contributing factors, in hauntings that occur are: tragic and untimely deaths, wrongful deaths, and even the conjuring of negative spirits by various groups and means. The Willows Weep house, seems to have several of the factors, that are considered prime causes of possible hauntings. Many psychics and investigators alike, who have visited the house, feel very strongly, that the house has a portal or a doorway in it, that allows all sorts of energies to flow throw it -- some good, but mostly bad. Some feel the house itself was built to funnel energy through it. Spirits or entities, being made of pure energy, are a most likely source for this energy.

Other outside events, that have occurred near the area, could also play a part in negative energies that are thought to be the cause of malevolent or negative-type hauntings. One example of this, is the case of a man named Watson. He was executed on April 3, 1879, for the murder of Ezra Compton, over a bar of soap. He was hanged at the old Newport jail and was interred in Helt's Prairie Cemetery. This is the only known, capital-punishment case, to have taken place in the county as of today. An execution by hanging, is a type of death that could cause a negative haunting, and it is possible that the energy created by that hanging, looms dark over the county. If the house is a doorway, as so many feel, then is it possible that Mr. Watson's spirit could have made its way to the house?

Still, there are far worse scenarios that have occurred, in and around the Vermillion County area, that could have created a venue for wandering or negative spirits to come through the portal that lies within Willows Weep. It is believed by many, that the original builder of the house, or others who lived in the house many years later, were into some sort of witchcraft in the house. The reasons for this are: the shape of the house, plus the weird, pointed structures protruding from the ceiling — that are above what was once the original four entrances and exits of the house — as well as the weird pamphlet that was found buried between the old original floor and the new laminate flooring. The pamphlet seems to be from a Christian organization called "The Church of God," however, it sports an upside-down pentacle on the cover. It also talks about how to communicate with spirits and summon the dead. In my opinion, this is some sort of cult masquerading as a Christian organization. Also, if it were a true Christian pamphlet, why would it be hidden away and buried between the old floor and new floor? This leads me into, an even more heinous aspect, that is going on in Indiana, and many other locations around the world. The fact of the matter is that Satanism, human sacrifice, and satanic ritual abuse are rampant around the world and in Indiana as well.

Looking into the possible dark witchcraft aspect of this case, I began to discover that there are a high number of Satanic-practicing covens in the state of Indiana. It was very eye- opening to see that the "Satanic Temple" is an Adopt-a-Highway sponsor (sign is along state route 421 in Boone County). Obviously, this fact doesn't mean that the "Satanic Church" has anything to do with the activity that occurs in the Willows Weep house. I'm just making an observation of the area, and that it is possible, even probable, that at sometime in the house's history, some type of witchcraft or ritualistic practices may have occurred in the house. When there are dark practices involved in any area, the odds drastically increase, that something may have been conjured into a location, either purposely or accidentally by unknowing victims.

Another prime example of the "Church of Satan" being prevalent in Indiana, is a very brutal satanic killing, that occurred in DeKalb County, Indiana, in 1991, in rural Auburn. This is but one of numerous, documented, Satanic-related killings in Indiana. In 1991 and 1992, a grisly murder involving carnival workers and Satanism saturated news headlines. Four men, who were working for amusement companies, at the "DeKalb County Free Fall Fair" in Auburn, were all involved in satanic practices. One of their coworkers, whose last name was Ault, expressed interest in joining the satanic church. According to testimony, from members of the group, during their murder trials, Ault knew about a previous murder that, a member of the group, had committed in Ohio. The group decided to scare him, in order to keep him quiet about the murder.

In September of 1991, the group searched for a secluded place, in which to indoctrinate Ault into the satanic church. Once they had completed work for the night, they headed to a very secluded farm building on Morningstar Road, north of Auburn. The men asked Ault to lie on a makeshift altar, after which they tied and gagged him. One of the men read an invocation to Satan. Using a knife, one of the men made a deep cut on Ault, from the neck to the stomach. Then the rest of men took turns making cuts to Ault's chest and abdomen, in the form of an inverted cross, as well as other cuts. Then the leader of the group asked Ault if he was ready to die, and as Ault answered, his throat was slit. His head and hands were removed and burned. The group then went and ate at a nearby restaurant in Auburn.

Another strange case, that occurred not far from Vermillion County, was the vicious kidnapping and murder, of a 12-year-old girl by the name of Shanda Sharer. She was tortured and burned to death in Madison, Indiana by four teenage girls. On the night of January 10, 1992, three of the girls — whose last names were Lawrence, Rippey, and Tackett — drove from Madison to the fourth girl's (Loveless's) house in New Albany. Once they arrived, they all borrowed clothes from Loveless. Loveless showed the group a knife and proclaimed that she was going to scare Sharer with it, because she disliked her for being a copycat, and stealing her girlfriend.

The four then drove to Jeffersonville, where they knew Sharer stayed with her father on the weekends. They arrived at Sharers' house just before dark. Loveless told Rippey and Lawrence to go up to the door and introduce themselves as friends of Amanda Heavrin, who was Loveless's former and Sharer's current girlfriend. Then they were to invite her to come with them, to visit Heavrin, who was waiting for them at the notorious "Witch's Castle," a stone house mostly in ruins, near the Ohio River.

Sharer wanted to go but her parents were awake, so she told the girls to come back around midnight. Loveless was furious at first, but two of the girls assured her they would come back for her. After attending a concert and participating in sexual relations with a couple of boys, the four girls again left for Sharer's house. Loveless made it clear that she couldn't wait to kill Sharer. While two of the girls went to retrieve Sharer from her home, Loveless hid under a blanket in the back seat of the car with the knife.

Rippey told Sharer, that her girlfriend Heavrin, was still waiting for her at the Witch's Castle, as Sharer was still reluctant to go with the group. Soon she decided to go with them. Once in the car, Rippey began questioning her about her relationship with Heavrin. That is when Loveless sprang out from under the blanket, quickly placing the knife to Sharer's throat and questioning her about her sexual relationship with Heavrin. As they drove towards the "Witch's Castle," Tackett told about the legend of the castle: that it was said to be owned by nine witches, and the townspeople had burned down the house, to rid the town of the witches' evil.

Once they arrived at the castle, they jerked the now-crying Sharer inside the castle and bound her legs and arms with rope. She was now being taunted by the group with threats of cutting her hair. Her jewelry was removed and they claimed the castle was full of bodies and she would be next. Going a step further, a T-shirt was removed and set on fire, for more intimidation. Fearing the flames would be spotted by passersby, they left the area with Sharer.

Begging and pleading with the girls to just take her home, Sharer was ordered by Loveless to remove her bra, after which Rippey slid off her bra and replaced it with Sharer's bra. Becoming lost two times, the group had to stop and ask for directions; all the while Sharer was bound and hidden under a blanket in the car. Finally, the car arrived near the woods close to Tackett's home in Madison.

Moving the victim to a remote garbage dump near a logging road, Lawrence and Rippey became scared and stayed in the car. Loveless and Tackett made Sharer strip completely, at which time Loveless beat her with her fists. Next, Loveless slammed her face into her knee, which caused cuts in her mouth from her own braces. Then Loveless attempted to cut Sharer's throat, but the knife was not sharp enough. Rippey got out of the car, to help hold her down, as Tackett and Loveless took turns stabbing her in the chest. As if this wasn't enough, they then strangled her with a rope until she went unconscious. Thinking she was dead, they put her in the trunk of the car.

Now driving to Tackett's house, the group went inside and cleaned themselves up, stopping to enjoy a beverage. Suddenly they heard Sharer screaming in the trunk of the car. Tackett retrieved a pairing knife and headed out to the car, stabbing her several more times, and coming back covered in blood. Tackett, in true negative witchcraft form, then told the girls' futures with her Rune stones. Later, around 2:30 a.m., Tackett and Loveless decided to go "country cruising" as they called it, while Rippey and Lawrence stayed behind. As Loveless and Tackett drove, they began hearing Sharer, crying and making gurgling noises in the trunk. Tackett stopped the car and the two opened the trunk. As Sharer sat up, covered in blood and unable to speak, Tackett grabbed a tire iron and beat her until she was silent, telling Loveless to smell it.

Returning to Tackett's house just before daybreak to clean up once again, Rippey asked about Sharer and the two of them described the torture, laughing about it. The commotion woke up Tackett's mother, and the girl told her mom, she would take the other girls home. Driving to a burn pile, they opened the trunk and sprayed Sharer with Windex saying, "You're not looking too hot now are you?"

Driving to a gas station to fill up the car with gas, Tackett also purchased a bottle of Pepsi. She dumped the cola out and replaced it with gas. The group then drove to a remote place off of U.S. Route 421, wrapped Sharer in a blanket still alive, and carried her to a field. Tackett ordered Rippey to pour the gas on her. Then they set her on fire. Loveless was not yet convinced she was dead, so they retrieved more gas and added it to the fire.

Afterward, the girls ate breakfast at a McDonald's, where they sat around joking how Sharer's body resembled one of the sausages they were eating. It wasn't long before the group began to talk about the murder. Their friends were reluctant to believe the story, until Tackett showed them the bloody trunk of the car. The rest is history. All the girls were convicted of murder and sentenced to various lengthy sentences.

With such senseless acts of violence and murder taking place, and the reference to witchcraft during many murders such as this one, investigators have to take a hard look at these evil acts, as a possible evil influences, controlling these people, having them do what a normal person would never dream of doing to another human being.

CHAPTER 23
WITCH'S CASTLE

UTICA, INDIANA

Having had supposed connections to the "Witch's Castle," the Sharer case is both disturbing and compelling, in that it prompts the question: Was it mere coincidence that Sharer's murder involved mention of this castle? Or was there some deep, dark, malevolent force, that lurks in the castle, that is drawing this sort of thing to it, like the Willows Weep house? In my opinion, there is little room for these things to all be mere happenstance.

The Witch's Castle legend says that a coven of witches once lived there a long time ago. It is said that the locals didn't like the women, so they burned them out, causing a curse to be placed on the town and people by the witches.

A paranormal investigator, believes that the structure, is experiencing a lot of paranormal activity. On one trip to the castle, she saw a woman dressed in old-style clothing, which surprised her. The investigator, asked others who were with her, if they could see this woman as well, and they replied they could not. Wanting to make contact with the woman, she walked toward the apparition, only to see the ghost vanish before her very eyes.

On another visit, the investigator and her husband heard crying over a device they were using. At the same time, her husband spotted an eight-foot-tall shadow figure. He approached the shadow figure, as his wife yelled at him not to touch it. The dark figure vanished and the crying stopped.

The investigator's experiences at the Witches' Castle left her desperate for more information. She wandered through the town of Utica, knocking on doors and seeking people who could talk about the property. She found an older man, who she says, is now dead. The man said he knew the original owners of the Witch's Castle, also known as "Mistletoe Falls." He said he also had heard of another legend, about a murder that had taken place on the property, long before Druien bought it. The man told the investigator, that a young boy had once lived on the property with his parents. A robber from a nearby area invaded their home, killing the boy's mother and father. Many years later, the boy grew up and the robber was executed for other crimes. Still wanting revenge, the boy kidnapped seven members of the robber's family and kept them prisoner at his old family home. Then one day, he hung all the family members and shot himself. Some believe, the seven victims' souls, are trapped to this day in the Witch's Castle and the boy is now the malevolent shadow person, who turned evil, because of his vengeful deed.

This chain of events, is exactly the kind of thing, that leaves a stain in the very ground where these events transpired. And if not cleansed or healed, it will leave an open wound for evil to fester and become even more prevalent. Just like Willows Weep.

CHAPTER 24
THE CASE OF IRENE RAY

The Ray family moved to Rochester, Indiana and settled in a shanty on the outskirts of town. Not having much money, the family soon applied for and were given welfare support. They were placed in a house on Audubon Street, where their neighbors soon came to resent them. Many of the residents were poor as well and couldn't stomach the fact that outsiders were being given assistance. The Ray family began to be harassed and the rumors began to fly.

It was thought, that maybe, Irene Ray started the rumors of witchcraft, as a way to scare people away, relieving her family from taunts and other attacks. No matter how the rumors started, they soon spread like wildfire. At first, the townsfolk murmured about the witch, but after the sudden illness of Georgia Knight Conrad, those murmurs became shouts. Irene had been trying to purchase some antiques from Georgia and had made several visits to her house, to pressure, the 24-year-old, into selling them. On one of these visits, it is said that Irene slipped into Georgia's bedroom and plucked some hairs from her brush. When leaving, Irene pronounced, "You'll be sorry soon!" That evening, Georgia fell into a faint and was soon diagnosed as having a "leaking heart valve." It wasn't long before the family connected the dots.

Another alleged victim, of the reported witch, was the Chief of Police Clay Sheets. The chief oversaw the removal of Irene's granddaughter, from her home, due to charges against the "morals of the household." A few days later, Chief Sheets died, of what appeared to be, a heart attack.

In addition to human hearts, Irene was accused of hexing one man's crops. Mrs. Ray made a habit of taking a shortcut through a field owned by Mr. Castle, who didn't appreciate the alleged witch trespassing on his property. When he confronted her, she ran her eyes back and forth over the patch, until they had covered every inch of it. After this happened, according to Castle, no potatoes sprouted that spring.

Other accusations included Ray inducing insomnia, nervous indigestion, fires, floods, and more. The alleged methods of hexing ranged from using voodoo dolls to taking hairs of the victim, intertwining them with hairs from her cat, placing them in vinegar, and burying them.

The allegations against Irene Ray mounted, and police were increasingly pressured to charge her with witchcraft. Fortunately, unlike Salem, Massachusetts in 1692, Indiana had no laws against witchcraft. The state did have vagrancy laws, making it illegal to be homeless. Irene was charged with vagrancy and arrested, only to be released when she promised the new chief of police that she and her family would leave town.

INDIANA TOWN BANS 'WITCH'

Woman Must Leave Roches-ter to Allay Citizens' Witchcraft Fears.

On May 11, 1938, Irene Ray and her husband, Charles, were exiled from the town of Rochester, Indiana due to allegations, that Irene, was a practitioner of witchcraft and had hexed several townspeople. It was alleged that her hexes, had caused personal property damage, serious illness, and even death.

More than likely, poor Irene and her husband were victims of mean and intolerant people. But was it the people themselves who were calculating? Or were they being manipulated by something else, something that caused them to become mob-like and throw these people away like the trash, just because they were outsiders and poor?

CHAPTER 25
GONE BUT NOT FORGOTTEN

KEN "DOC" HEAD

In life you meet a lot of people; some of them leave a lasting impression on you. Ken was one of those people. I knew Ken from doing a few investigations with his group, ESP. I was fortunate enough to investigate with them a few times and we all became friends. On one occasion, they had invited me to investigate "St. Albans Asylum." I jumped at the chance for many reasons. They are great investigators and also a joy to be around. We always had a great time, and seemed to capture great evidence, when we investigate together. The another big reason was that the location is awesome.

On this occasion, they had driven their motorhome all the way to Virginia from South Florida. After the investigation, we had sad our goodbyes and I headed home. I found out the next day, that the engine on the motorhome had blown and was shot. They ended up having to leave the RV in Virginia to get a brand, new engine.

After some time, Doc's wife Terri contacted me and said, "We have a proposal for you." I said, "Oh what's that?" She explained that the RV was fixed and asked if I would like to drive it to Savannah and investigate a location with them. They would take care of everything. I said it sure sounds like a plan. It was set. I drove my car to the location of the RV, jumped in and proceeded on my way to Savannah in a 30-plus-foot motor home.

Once there, we walked the streets of one of the most haunted cities in America, and stayed in a very haunted home in the historic district. We captured some great evidence.

Ken insisted that he pay me extra money for driving the RV down there. I refused to take it, but he would have nothing of me saying "no." That's the kind of guy he was.

He was a doctor who dedicated his life to healing sick people, and he will be missed by many. Ken, you are gone but not forgotten, my friend. See you on the other side!!

MICHELLE FITZPATRICK

While researching the house and property for this book, the former owner, Brenda Zimmerman Johnson, and a fellow investigator, Barry Gaunt, both informed me of another investigator had spent significant time investigating the house. They recommended that talk with her about some of her experiences and thoughts about the house.

Even though we had never met in person, I knew who Michelle Fitzpatrick was, through friends of friends and through the paranormal circles. I knew that she worked in law enforcement as I had, and she had quite a few years of experience in the paranormal field. I felt it was imperative that I speak with her about the house. Barry had made the connection for us. Within a day or two, we were on the phone discussing some of her experiences and what she felt may be going on there.

We spoke on the phone for a few hours that night and what she told me really grabbed my attention, because it was much different, than what I had heard from so many others I had interviewed about the house. Personally, I feel it is important to get as many different takes and views on a location as possible, so one can look at all of them, in an attempt to discover, what may be causing the phenomena, at any given location.

Once on the phone together, I could hear the excitement in her voice. I knew that she was going to be able to convey to me, what her experiences and thoughts on the house were. She started by telling me that she was fascinated with this location, but at the same time very afraid of it. She as especially fearful since her last investigation there, as she felt that something had attacked her, in a spiritual way. She said that she had been having nightmares about it, for quite sometime, after she had last investigated the house. She also said, within the first five minutes of our conversation, "You have one hell of a location there" but she was stern with what she said after that. She exclaimed, and I'll never forget this, that the place is "PURE EVIL!"

I wanted her to elaborate as to why she thought that, and I wanted her to tell me what she thought was causing the phenomena in the house. She went on to say that she didn't think it was a normal haunting, caused by human spirits, or even your run-of- the-mill demonic type of entities. I was a bit taken back and wondered what she meant by this. She explained that she felt there was definitely a doorway, that things were coming through there, but it was more like a portal to a different dimension. She felt that creatures, from a different dimension, were coming in and out of it, causing horrible things to happen to people in the house. I was a bit flabbergasted at this, but wanted her to go on about it.

She claimed that these creatures were coming to her in dreams, and had even visited her at her home, on more than one occasion. She had some trouble describing them, but said they were very similar, to what we know as demons, only they were coming from another dimension. She said she knew this because they showed her, in her dreams, where they were coming from. I found this fascinating and a whole different viewpoint, on what others had described, as to what was happening at Willows Weep. We talked back and forth for a quite some time until, she said that she had to work the next day and we should continue the conversation later in the week. I concurred.

Before she hung up, she told me that she was going to share a bunch of her evidence with me, that she had collected from her investigations at the house. Some time went by and she finally messaged me. We both were busy with work and projects. She said she still had to find the evidence, she had obtained on the house, and that it wouldn't be much longer until she would get back with me on it. I had gotten called, to go film some episodes, for a couple of new Paranormal TV shows, and we made plans to talk when I got back from doing that.

I was getting ready to message her, on the weekend of February 22, 23, when I saw a post that she had passed away. I was dumbfounded! I quickly searched her social media page, where I found numerous posts confirming that from many people. I contacted our mutual friend, Barry Gaunt, and relayed what I had seen, as he was unaware of anything. He then got on the wire with mutual friends for more information. In a very short amount of time, it was confirmed, that she did in fact pass suddenly. I was very saddened by the unexpected turn of events. I am glad that we did get to talk about the house for a short time. I feel everyone meets for a reason. I want to wish her Godspeed and let her know she will be missed by many.

Investigators' Contact Information

Daywalkers' Bio

John and Debbie Holiday are a married couple that have 20-plus years of paranormal experience. Each brings a unique set of gifts to the field, which include abilities as empaths.

Each one can walk through a location and identify where the paranormal activity is, which may include knowing the gender of the ghosts in question and the reason for the activity.

Debbie Holiday works as a hospice caregiver and has helped many people to cross over from our world into the next.

John Holiday is retired, after working in social services, helping others to achieve a better life for themselves. John is also a paranormal author, writing several books that are available on Amazon.com.

The husband and wife team uses modern scientific equipment, such as the X-Cam SLS camera, REM Pods, EMF detectors, audio recorders, IR and digital cameras.

John and Debbie's approach is simple: by showing love and acceptance, they gain the trust of the spirit and better understanding of what is needed. Together, we are Daywalkers Paranormal Investigations.

NOT LONG AFTER INVESTIGATING WILLOWS WEEP IN 2019 JOHN AND DEBBIE RETIRED FROM THE PARANORMAL INVESTIGATION FIELD FOR PERSONAL HEALTH RELATED REASONS.

"The Original ParaSisters®"About

Ft. Wayne's Premier Paranormal Team! The Original ParaSisters® are an elite, female team, experienced and passionate paranormal investigators/ researchers. We are an experienced, professional and courteous group of individuals with a passion for paranormal research. We at all times respect our client's religious beliefs, and their property.

To contact, "The Original ParaSisters®" you will find us at the below-listed sites:

www.theoriginalparasisters.wordpress.com

To listen to our EVP'S, go to "ichaseshadows," at www.youtube.com

No Nonsense Paranormal About

Two teams joining forces on one paranormal project web series. Through audio and video evidence unlocking the afterlife one door at a time. https://m.me/Nononsenceparanormalproject?
fbclid=IwAR2JvIxLPSBL28-7P_3AqyJ-
eVBGpxfdeR_9KrBaNHVG52qvXAGZgCflJMU

Explorers Of Spirit Phenomena About

ESP, El Con Society of the Paranormal was formed in 2009 by Dr. John Head and Terri Rohde. In 2015 we became a member of True Ghost Stories TV Series, Team Florida. In 2016 ESP transformed into Explorers of Spirit Phenomena. ESP's mission is to bridge the gap between the living world and the spirit world. We embrace the opportunity we have been given.

Terri Rohde is the team's co-founder, case manager and lead investigator. She moved from Connecticut to Florida in 1973. She obtained her bachelor's degree in Education from USF and her master's degree from Nova Southeastern University. She works as an author, librarian, teacher and medical assistant. She's been attempting communication with the spirit world, since she was a child ,and has always felt very connected to that world.

Tracy Watts is the team's videographer and investigator. She is a fifth generation Floridian. She obtained her bachelor's degree in education, and her master's degree in Library and Information Science from USF. She began her career teaching emotionally disturbed children and presently works as a library media specialist. Her first paranormal experience as a child occurred less than a mile from the team's home base.

Contact-http://www.espexplorers.com/contact.html

Nicole Novell Info

Paranormal Investigator, Radio Show Host~ LP Spotlight Radio Tues @10:30pm ~Live Streamed Paranormal Investigations- @NikiParaUnNormal on Facebook for info

Research Credits

Dave Spinks, Nicole Novelle, Brenda Zimmerman Johnson, Barry Gaunt, Melvin Brazzell, Elaine Brannon. Thanks to all of you for your time effort and contributions to this work.

"Necromancy," Entry 1. *Webster's Dictionary.* Web. August 3, 2019.

ABOUT THE AUTHOR

DAVE SPINKS

After having a terrifying encounter with a bigfoot, with his paternal grandfather, and a few years later experiencing an after-death visit from his maternal grandfather, Dave Spinks became fascinated by the paranormal and started his search for answers.

Gathering evidence in the form of EVPs, video, photographic data and personal experiences, Dave collected experiences from many different people from all walks of life to include: law enforcement officers, farmers, hunters, schoolteachers, doctors and more. Dave cites "In Search Of," with Leonard Nimoy and Hans Holzer, as one of his many early Influences.

As an adult, he joined the USAF right out of college and became a trained observer. He spent eight years active duty and one in the Army National Guard. His service in the military gave him the opportunity to investigate locations in Italy while stationed there from 1997 through 2001.

After the military, Dave pursued a career in law enforcement, working for the West Virginia Department of Corrections for two years and moving into federal law enforcement with the U.S. Department of Justice for another eight years.

His professional path greatly enhanced his investigative skills. During his years working in the federal and state government, he continued his pursuit of the supernatural, investigating and researching any time he had an opportunity.

In 2011, he retired from law enforcement and decided to dive headlong into the pursuit of the paranormal on a full-time basis. Since that time, he has worked alongside some of the most well-known names in the various fields of the paranormal, including John Zaffis, Rosemary Ellen Guiley, David Weatherly, Ross Allison, Eric Altman, Barry Gaunt, and many more.

In fact, Dave became great friends with David Weatherly after they met in 2013. The two of them founded the "Society of the Supernatural" in the hopes of bringing together people with vast experience, in the fields as a collective, to move the field forward. The two are constantly using new, innovative techniques and equipment in the search for answers. They are constantly conducting investigations, adding to their knowledge and experiences.

Dave has investigated, researched, and written about a variety of topics to include: cryptids, hauntings and ufology. He has been a featured speaker at numerous conferences around the country, and is often asked to lecture on a variety of paranormal topics. He has been a featured guest on countless radio shows and paranormal podcasts from around the world, including "Coast to Coast AM," "Spaced Out Radio," and "Arcane Radio," to name a few.

Dave has appeared on several television shows, including Destination America's "Terror in the Woods," the Travel Channel's "These Woods are Haunted," the Travel Channel's "Paranormal 911" and "In Search of Monsters," and various episodes of the History Channel's "The UneXplained." In 2018, he was featured in the film by Small Town Monsters "The Flatwoods Monster: A legacy of Fear."

Dave Spinks has also coproduced several investigation videos on DVD, including: "Point Pleasant Files Vol. 1," "Haunting of Sweet Springs," "Ghost of the Guyer Opera House 1699," "A Haunting in Bellaire," and "House of Haunted Fields."

Dave's books include "West Virginia Bigfoot," "The 'Real West Virginia Hauntings'" a series, "Real West Virginia UFO's", and "Willows Weep." He has also contributed to the wildly popular "Wood Knocks" series by David Weatherly. Dave has several new works in progress so be on the lookout for those as well.

"I love to share what I do with others, in the hopes of answering some of man's greatest questions: Is there life after death? Are there unknown creatures walking among us? Are we alone in the universe? I believe there is something after death. We are not alone, and that there are unknown creatures walking among us. Finding answers is my motivation."

TO CONNECT WITH DAVE ONLINE
&
INQUIRE ABOUT EVENT BOOKINGS
http://www.davespinksparanormalinvestigator.com
https://www.facebook.com/DaveSpinksRealSupernatural/
https://www.facebook.com/societysupernatural/

Made in the USA
Monee, IL
20 November 2023

46978485R00092